Returning to the Land of Oz

Finding hope, love, and courage on your yellow brick road

John A. Tamiazzo, PhD

Edited by
Linda Ulvaeus

Bibliographical Note: This book includes
7 original drawings by W.W. Denslow that
appeared in the original 1900 edition, utilizing
only their black line elements.

Eloquent Books

Eloquent Books
An imprint of Strategic Book Group
PO Box 333
Durham, CT 06422
www.strategicbooks.com

ISBN: 978-1-60911-409-1

This book is dedicated to those who
have seen and loved the film
The Wizard of Oz
and to those who have read and enjoyed
L. Frank Baum's
The Wonderful Wizard of Oz.

Contents

The Wizard of Oz is not just a charming children's book or a highly entertaining film. Within the story line of this seemingly simple tale, Baum gave us one of the greatest resources for personal transformation ever written.

Introduction

Returning to the Land of Oz

1939 WAS HERALDED BY FILM CRITICS as the 'golden year' for film. Classics such as *Mr. Smith Goes to Washington, Wuthering Heights, the Hunchback of Notre Dame, Goodbye, Mr. Chips,* and Oscar winner for best picture *Gone with the Wind,* captivated adult audiences in movie houses across America. But, another film was released in 1939 which became the most popular and loved family film of all time. That film was *The Wizard of Oz.*

The Wizard of Oz was based upon the book, *The Wonderful Wizard of Oz,* written by L. Frank Baum in 1900. It won best children's book both in 1900 and 1901. The film, *The Wizard of Oz,* which has been seen by over 2 billion people world-wide, brings the book to life with magical characterizations, unforgettable songs, and fabulous dance sequences and choreography. One of the most wonderful additions to the story made by the screen writers is Judy Garland singing *Somewhere Over the Rainbow.*

Ranked as the greatest movie song of all time by the American Film Institute and the National Endowment of Arts, *Somewhere Over the Rainbow* touched film goers unlike any song had in many years. When people heard Judy Garland tenderly sing it, they understood the power and magic of its lyrics. Millions of Americans were still out of work as the country continued recovering from the devastating effects of The Great Depression. People went to movie houses to enter into a fantasy world for a few hours and perhaps be transported to a place far, far away where troubles melt like lemon drops. *The Wizard of Oz* provided them with that place.

Baum's background provides important insights about the creation of his book. Baum had an exceptionally kind and loving nature, an extraordinary imagination, and an excellent sense of humor. He was very sociable and loved talking to people. He believed in the power of magic, which he thought could be used for good or for evil depending upon the disposition of the person practicing it.

He wanted to be a journalist and spent much of his adult life writing for many prominent publications, including the Chicago Evening Post. As a journalist, he developed excellent writing skills. His talent for writing combined with his vivid imagination led to the publication of 6 children's books including *Phunnyland, Mother Goose in Prose* and 13 sequels to the *The Wizard of Oz*. He also wrote 55 novels and 82 short stories.

In 1892 Baum joined the Theosophical Society in Chicago. Theosophy must have had a powerful influence on the development of his imagination because Theosophy avows the belief in a reality beyond the physical world which includes spirits and the afterlife. Theosophy espouses universal brotherhood and sisterhood and the importance of developing balance and harmony within one's self and in the world around. The focus of Theosophy is the search for and discovery of truth. All of these are uplifting themes in *The Wizard of Oz*.

Baum went to the Chicago World Expo in 1893 and the design of the city there, the White City, was purportedly the inspiration for the Emerald City. Baum was an excellent observer of life, always remembered what inspired him, and put these memories into his stories.

Baum's mother-in-law, a devout feminist and leader who marched with Susan B. Anthony and Elizabeth Cady Stanton, founded the Women's National Liberal Union. This union was dedicated to the separation of church and state and focused on social reform. Baum was an advocate of women's suffrage and the women's rights movement. As a journalist, he wrote extensively about the fundamental need for women's rights and marched alongside his wife and mother-in-law to that end.

It was not uncommon to find Baum telling his stories to an enthralled audience of girls and boys. Groups of children, including his sons, gathered in his office and listened to his imaginative tale about Dorothy and her friends in the magical Land of Oz. There is much speculation about how Baum came up with the title, *The Wonderful Wizard of Oz*. It was not his first choice. The original title was The Emerald City. Supposedly, the inspiration for the location of his story came to him as he looked at one of his file cabinets labeled O-Z. Baum was an exceptionally creative man and it is just as plausible that the title came to him in a dream, a day dream, or intuitively while passionately telling the story to a spellbound group of children.

Throughout the entire story, Dorothy, the Scarecrow, the Tin Woodman, and the Lion consistently solve difficulties by drawing upon their own courage, enterprise, imagination, and intuition. With the help she gets from others, Dorothy is able to successfully maneuver through the unfamiliar and unpredictable

Land of Oz. She has an indomitable will and stands up for herself, defying those who act threateningly and irrationally. Because Baum whole-heartedly believed in the equality of women, Dorothy is a celebration of the empowerment of the feminine spirit. In Dorothy, Baum most likely created the courageous and compassionate daughter he always wanted.

Returning to the Land of Oz explores and examines both Baum's book and the 1939 film. The film added dialogue and scenes that did not appear in the original book, and the book contained many important challenges that Dorothy, the Scarecrow, the Tin Woodman, and the Lion faced, that were not portrayed in the film.

The Wizard of Oz is not just a charming children's book or a highly entertaining film. Within the story line of this seemingly simple tale, Baum gave us one of the greatest resources for personal transformation ever written.

Sigmund Freud, who was born just 9 days before Baum, unlocked the door to the power of the unconscious, hypnosis, defense mechanisms, and to our inner world of dreams. C.G. Jung opened our eyes to the mystical realm, the collective unconscious, symbolism, archetypes, the complexities and structure of the psyche, and the integration of the masculine and feminine principles. Abraham Maslow made us aware of the importance of a healthy Psychology built upon the foundations of love, belonging, creativity, and peak experiences. Baum took all of these intricate and dynamic areas of study, simplified them, and brought them to life in the form of a fun and enchanting story with an innocent young girl as the protagonist. He added a little dog to comfort her, and six colorful characters (the Scarecrow, the Tin Woodman, the Lion, the Wizard, and two Witches) to spar and interact with. Given all of its brilliant theories and complex terminology, the field of Psychology has not provided us with better insights for successfully making personal changes than the *The Wizard of Oz*.

The Wizard of Oz teaches us about using our minds creatively in solving problems and handling adversity. It helps us to understand the value of service to others and assisting those in need and distress. It shows us why it is important to love, to let go of the past, and to open our hearts. It demonstrates how to defy our fears and to draw upon our inner courage and resourcefulness. It encourages us to speak up for ourselves, to stand up to those who threaten us, and to move forward despite life's obstacles and challenges. It illustrates the importance of working in harmony with others toward achieving goals that are important to us. Through song, dance, and endearing characterizations, it magically portrays the power of imagination, intuition, and the enchantment of play.

One of the most interesting twists in the story is reflected in the title, which emphasizes the Wizard rather than Dorothy. *The Wizard of Oz* could have easily been called Dorothy's Journey to the Land of Oz. But Baum wanted the characters and the reader to be dramatically led to The Wizard only to be deeply disappointed and outraged by what is ultimately discovered. In that momentous part of the story we uncover something quite miraculous about the resiliency of human nature, something that the more progressive schools of Psychology have attempted to teach us and Baum's tale so cleverly illustrated over a hundred years ago.

Somewhere, over the rainbow, way up high
There's a land that I heard of once in
a lullaby.
Somewhere, over the rainbow, skies are blue
And the dreams that you dare to dream
Really do come true.
Someday I'll wish upon a star and wake up
Where the clouds are far behind me.
Where troubles melt like lemon drops,
Away above the chimney tops
That's where you'll find me.
Somewhere, over the rainbow, blue birds fly.
Birds fly over the rainbow,
Why then—oh why can't I?

E.Y. Harburg

Chapter One

Somewhere Over the Rainbow

WITHIN MINUTES OF LISTENING TO DOROTHY sing *Somewhere Over the Rainbow,* we watch her being whisked away in her little house by a great cyclone. In the film version, Dorothy is hit in the head by a flying window that has become unhinged by the force of nature, but in the original story, *The Wonderful Wizard of Oz,* L. Frank Baum describes this scene quite differently,

"The north and south winds met where the house stood and made it the exact center of the cyclone. It was a gentle ride and Dorothy felt like she was being rocked like a baby in a cradle. Sometimes she worried about being dashed to pieces, but she resolved to wait calmly to see what the future would bring. In spite of the swaying of the house and the wailing of the wind, Dorothy soon closed her eyes and fell fast asleep."

Dorothy is suddenly awakened from her sleep as the house makes contact with the earth. When Dorothy looks out the window, she discovers she is in a most beautiful and colorful place. She walks outside and is immediately greeted by the Good Witch of the North, Glinda, who asks her if she is a good witch or a bad witch. Dorothy is confused by the question. Glinda tells her that her house has landed on the Wicked Witch of the East instantly killing her. As a result, all the Munchkins are now free. In honor of this surprising incident, the Munchkins celebrate and Dorothy is given the Wicked Witch's Ruby Red Shoes, originally Silver in Baum's 1900 book.

Dorothy is appreciative of the Munchkins' excitement and the Good Witch's gift, but all she really wants is to go back home to Kansas. She is told that perhaps the Wizard of Oz can be of assistance to her. The Good Witch directs Dorothy to the Yellow Brick Road, kisses her on the forehead, and says, "No one will dare harm a person who has been kissed by the Witch of the North."

Glinda instinctively knows that Dorothy needs a lot of support to make her journey to Oz as successful as possible. The Good Witch, in her kind way, gives her love and the hope that the Wizard of Oz will help her get back home. The Good Witch clearly tells Dorothy that she is protected by her kiss and that no harm will come to her. Glinda gives Dorothy what every parent needs to give a child, the feeling of being safe.

Feeling safe is extremely important in life. Without safety, trust does not develop. One builds upon the foundation of the other. Many of us have trust issues because we didn't experience safety within our home and family. Perhaps we didn't have good role models, didn't have people we could count on, were frightened often, or weren't allowed to really be a child in full innocence because of the demands made on us. Perhaps we didn't have a soothing voice to listen to that conveyed the message and suggestion again and again that we were safe and nothing would harm us.

As a guest speaker, a very successful greeting card designer and author named Flavia spoke at one of my Psychology of Creativity classes. She told us a wonderful story about the power of positive suggestion. Her Uncle Jack had always told her that one of the secrets of life is to listen to the right voice. When a voice says you are stupid, untalented, unattractive, or a failure, you are listening to the wrong voice. If a voice says you are alone, helpless, or you don't deserve good things to happen to you, it is the wrong voice to listen to. When a voice says you are lovely, safe, talented, free to choose, and offers hope, THAT is the right voice to listen to!

One day on a street in Los Angeles, Flavia was trying to sell her art and no one seemed interested. An inner voice said that doing this 'art thing' was a waste of time and that Flavia needed to get a real job. She remembered the origin of this voice, what her Uncle Jack had told her, and realized, like Dorothy listening to the voice of the Wicked Witch, that this voice was the wrong one to listen to. She knew it was the wrong voice because of how she felt. Shortly thereafter, a man came by and told Flavia that she was a very talented artist and he proceeded to buy every painting she was selling. She knew his was the right voice to listen to because of the good feelings that arose within her. This 'ray of hope' that came along gave her the confidence to take the next steps as an artist and greeting card designer. Within a few years, she was running one of the largest greeting card companies in the USA.

The Good Witch's voice is the right one for Dorothy to listen to because it conveys the supportive message she needs to get through the Land of Oz safely. Because of the things Glinda says and the way she says them, Dorothy goes on her journey to Oz feeling optimistic, fully expecting that the Wizard will grant her wish.

When Dorothy wakes up after the cyclone has passed, her world is turned upside down. When awful or unexpected things happen in life, many of us just want 'to go back home' to the way things were. It is basic to human nature to hold on to the things that are familiar; to embrace the known. But, sometimes life has its own agenda and causes things to happen that are beyond our control: the divorce, the illness, the death, the accident, the job loss, the fire, the economic downturn. Sometimes the things and people we have always counted on are no longer there! During these very challenging times we are left with the resources that no one can take away from us: our minds, our imaginations, our hearts, our faith, our dreams, our hopes, our aspirations, and our perseverance.

In the opening scenes of the film, Dorothy sees the grayness of the Kansas prairie all around her. She knows how hard her uncle and aunt work to keep the farm prosperous and she also notices that Uncle Henry and Aunt Em never laugh. The hard life on the farm has sapped all the joy out of both of them. Dorothy hopes for a better life for herself and for her little dog. She looks up towards the sky and sings her classic song, *Somewhere over the Rainbow*. A few minutes later, the storm arrives and Dorothy is sucked up into the force of the cyclone and transported from the known to the unknown.

Baum wrote, "The sun shone bright and the birds sang sweet and Dorothy did not feel nearly as bad as you might think a little girl would who had been suddenly whisked away from her own country and set down in the midst of a strange land."

Dorothy's belief that the Wizard of Oz is going to help her get back home is the driving force that propels her entire journey. Nothing dissuades her from this vision. Her first wish has come true, she is now somewhere over the rainbow and has her loving companion Toto at her side. But now she has a second wish: to see the Wizard of Oz. As she takes each step on the yellow bricks, I would venture a guess that she hears Glinda's encouraging voice again and again: "No one will dare harm a person who has been kissed by the Witch of the North."

*Once upon a time a mind got stuck.
It got stuck in a thought that life was
difficult. It got stuck in a thought that
it lacked something. It got stuck in a
thought that something was wrong.
The thought deepened and it spread
into a belief that the mind wasn't OK.
Seeing no way out, the mood darkened
and the mind was swept up in a
whirlwind of fear.*

*Exhausted, the mind fell into a deep
sleep and had a most amazing dream.
In the dream a calming voice said to
simply relax and to trust that everything
would be OK for there was a Higher
Intelligence at work. Upon awakening
the mind felt hopeful, something it
hadn't felt in a very long time.*

Chapter Two

If Only I had a Brain

SOMETIMES LIFE IS JUST PLAIN DIFFICULT and presents us with more challenges than we had expected. We feel stuck but don't know how to get unstuck. We feel lonely but don't know who to turn to for comfort. We're afraid but don't know who to reach out to for help. We're lost but don't know how to find our way home.

One of the first people Dorothy meets on her journey is a Scarecrow who is stuck on a pole. When he finds out that Dorothy is on her way to see the Wizard and to ask him to help her get back to Kansas, he wonders if the Great Wizard might also help him by giving him some brains.

Baum wrote, "I don't want people to call me a fool, and if my head stays stuffed with straw instead of with brains, as yours is, how am I ever to know anything?"

Sometimes it seems like our heads are stuffed with straw and we are unable to think clearly. Sometimes our minds are muddled with conflicting thoughts and negative words and images. Sometimes we are so confused that we make irrational decisions and unhealthy mistakes.

Our thoughts set the tone for the feelings we have and the experiences that come our way.

Scarecrow thinks he is stupid and doesn't have a brain. There are millions of people in the world who supposedly have brains, but cannot be swayed to think reasonably, to act responsibly, or to do something which is going to improve the quality of life here.

Baum wrote, "How can you talk if you don't have brains?" asked Dorothy.

"I don't know," responded the Scarecrow. "Some people without brains do an awful lot of talking, don't they?"

What the Scarecrow really wants is to think of himself in a more positive light. He wants to know he is a person of substance and not just a fool stuffed with straw. Once Dorothy physically removes him from the pole and he becomes unstuck, he knows he is in the presence of someone who really cares. He knows he has met someone who can help him achieve his goal. With a kind gesture and words of encouragement, she helps him see a bright future. As a result, his trust in her is immediate and he joins with her on her journey without hesitation.

We all need these kinds of relationships in life. We need good people to influence us and creative thinkers to open the way to a realm of possibilities. We need people who know where they are going to help us find our way. We need to spend time with inspirational people so we too can be inspired. We need to spend time with caring people so we can learn how to self nurture and learn how to give. We need to spend time with people who make us laugh so we can develop a sense of humor. We need to spend more time with people who open doors and awaken our optimism. We need to spend time with people who have brains and who use their minds in imaginative ways. We need to spend time with people who lighten our steps.

The Scarecrow intuitively knows that Dorothy is a person of great integrity. She is taking him on a life changing journey and not just for a ride. Dorothy opens the Scarecrow's imagination to a vision that is so beautiful, that in that moment his life is changed forever. Once Dorothy releases the Scarecrow from the pole, she too is released and free. When we open the door to freedom for those that are stuck and in distress, we also free ourselves. What we extend to others comes back to us again and again.

The Scarecrow tells Dorothy of a conversation he had with a crow. The crow told him that all he needs is a brain and he would be "as good a man as any of them and a better man than some of them." After the crow flew away, he decided to try and get some brains. Shortly thereafter, he met Dorothy.

Life is like this. Once we make a decision to improve our lives in some way and this decision is made from a place of integrity, chances are good that opportunity will open the door to our request. The key word here is 'integrity.' Integrity is without blame, judgment or resentment. Integrity does not harbor arrogance or guilt. Integrity arises from an inner wisdom and a place inside that reflects higher values and optimistic beliefs. These are not necessarily the ones that were passed down to us from our parents or that we learned along the way, but they are the ones that are positive, that will lighten our steps, give us confidence, and fill us with vitality.

Like the Scarecrow, when we have an inner thought, vision, or intention and a person or situation comes along that highlights and mirrors that thought, vision, or intention, this is called synchronicity. Synchronicities can be viewed as miracles. We cannot logically explain how or why synchronicities or miracles occur but we can say they happen because of divine intervention, destiny, or because we pay attention and are open to them occurring. Life brings us extraordinary experiences and gifts that defy our ability to fully understand how it all works. One of these miraculous gifts is our brain.

The brain is composed of over 100 billion brain cells. This remarkable and elaborate communication system controls, coordinates and regulates all the physical and mental activities we perform each day. Every action we take, every step, every gesture, every breath, every thought, every word we express, our senses, creativeness, the decisions we make, and the memories we store and retrieve require the direction, orchestration, and responsiveness of our miraculous brain. The Scarecrow wants a brain. To him it seems like such a simple wish.

Brain cells communicate by releasing chemicals allowing an impulse to pass from one cell to another. What we think and the imagery we entertain directly affect the chemistry of the brain. The food we eat, like the thoughts we engage in, either support the healthy functioning of the brain or deprive it of the nutrients it needs. When we see and appreciate things of beauty our brain releases chemicals that support the good feelings associated with what we see. When we hear the sound of pleasing music our brain releases chemicals that create feelings of pleasure. The memories we entertain and the future imagery we engage in immediately impact the neurotransmitters the brain releases. We, therefore, have the power to positively alter our brain chemistry. The important things to keep in mind are what we feed it, how we use it, and the ways we care for our miracle brain.

The Scarecrow knows he wants a brain, but a deeper look reveals that what he really wants is an intelligent and fully-functioning brain that will support him in life, a brain that can discern truth from untruth, a brain that will lift him up above the doldrums, a brain that will open the way for fulfilling life experiences.

The Scarecrow is off to a good start. He is no longer stuck on a pole and now he finds himself walking on very solid ground. He is joined by a delightful companion who is protected from danger and wears a pair of magical Ruby Red Shoes. He is on the way to Oz to meet the Wizard and have his wish granted. His future is looking very bright indeed.

Envisioning and imagining a positive future is very healing. When we visually see the future successfully unfolding and feel this success kinesthetically in every part of our bodies, the universe responds. Positive things happen.

"The imagination has power and genius in it," wrote Einstein. He once told a story about a dream he had as a child in which he rode a sled down a snowy mountain at such high speed that the stars and planets began to revolve backwards as they made their way through the heavens. He said that he meditated on this dream often, and his deep reflection led to his theories of special and general relativity.

In her book *Wisdom of the Psyche*, Ginette Paris writes, "Depression's opposite is not happiness; it is rather a state where imagination comes alive." Imagination is always our way out of whatever is making us feel trapped. Imagination offers us possibilities, opens doors, and helps us to reach beyond the places where we may be stuck. Imagination activates all of our senses so that we can see new opportunities, feel alive inside again, hear the music, smell the flowers, reinvent ourselves, and begin to take the steps which will lead us in a new direction.

Dorothy and the Scarecrow are on their way to see the Wizard of Oz. There is no hesitation, there are no doubts. They are inspired, excited, and single-minded in their respective goals. This positive and focused mindedness experienced again and again literally creates new neural pathways within the brain stimulating fresh patterns of thinking, feeling, and acting.

When Dorothy first looks into the eyes of the Scarecrow, the initial contact made by him is a wink. His wink awakens her curiosity. His wink lets her know that he is alive. His wink is a simple gesture that opens the way to communication between them.

We do this all the time. Our eyes connect with the eyes of another. We see someone and we smile. We extend our hand. We open our arms and lovingly embrace one another. We make a friendly gesture. We say something. These are all ways of making contact. Being able to communicate what we want, what we feel, what we know, what we would like to know, and where we want to go in life is essential to maintaining a healthy life style and developing successful relationships.

When I worked in community mental health facilities in the 70's and 80's, I spent my days with hundreds of so called 'seriously mentally ill' adults who were unable to make contact in the usual ways. In their fear, they recoiled into protective states where it appeared that communication was shut down. But when I really took the time to observe body language and took added measures to understand their metaphorical styles of communication, I discovered that they desperately wanted to make contact. They had simply lost the ability to do it in conventional ways. They were struggling. They had lost hope. They had shut down. They lived in constant fear and trepidation. Their lives had gotten completely out of balance.

Early on I discovered that I felt tremendous satisfaction in spending my days with them, finding ways to make contact, helping them to feel safe enough to slowly learn to trust me. Through books, poetry, discussions, yoga, walks, sports, dance, music, art, cooking, baking, writing, relaxation exercises, making pottery, and participating in drama groups, I gradually found creative and non threatening ways to connect with them, and ways for them to connect and communicate with me.

For our continued health and well-being, we need to create balance within our lives. This essential balance encompasses both the logical and imaginative, the mind and the heart. We need the ridiculous and the sublime, the studious and the playful, quality time with others and refreshing time alone, problem solving and activities that enliven the spirit. Creativity, for example, requires that we use both the practical and the imaginative modalities. The imaginative part of the psyche is where inspiration arises. We then take this inspiration, begin to work with it, shape and hone it into something new. When we watch a dancer passionately move across the stage, we must always remember that it took years of study and hundreds of hours of hard work to make her vision of dance something of beauty to behold.

Many of the patients I met in the psychiatric hospitals had creative minds but often couldn't take their ideas and use them in practical ways. They couldn't take a skill and use it to improve the quality of their lives. They had gifts, talents, and abilities, but were consumed by a maelstrom of fear. Like the Scarecrow, they were stuck until 'a Dorothy' appeared.

I heard a story about the eminent psychiatrist, Milton Erickson, who worked with a woman who had agoraphobia and was afraid to go out. When Erickson visited her in her home, he saw that the house was a mess and the woman was in a disheveled state. As he looked around, he noticed a beautiful African violet plant growing in the kitchen window. He pondered, "How could a woman who lives like this take care of a plant like that?" As they worked together, he inspired her to propagate African violet plants and to take them to hospitals and to homes of people who were confined. Many years later when she died, the local newspaper referred to her as the African Violet Queen who brought a smile to the faces of hundreds of people. The department of public social services had decreed that she was incapable of managing her own life. In spite of their assessment, she became a super star because one man noticed something about her that no one else perceived.

Like Milton Erickson, Dorothy pays attention and her curiosity is awakened. She feels Scarecrow's sadness and dissatisfaction and she reaches out. She removes the pole from his back and frees him from his confined life. Dorothy tells him of her dream of returning home, and in that moment he sees something he hasn't seen before. Like the African Violet Queen, he has a glimmer of hope and sees what is possible. Suddenly, his world begins to enlarge and the space he has been occupying opens up. In that moment, he trades the known for the unknown.

The unknown affects people differently. Some people get very excited about discovering the unknown because they enjoy learning something new and reinventing themselves. They like the challenge of doing something different. Others are overwhelmed by it until a Dorothy like-person comes along and rekindles their hope for the future. Hopeless thinking becomes hopeful thinking. What seemed unattainable is now within sight.

Dorothy, Toto, and the Scarecrow are on a journey to the Land of Oz. Nothing can stop them. The Wicked Witch will try. Natural barriers will stop their progress for awhile and all kinds of trouble will ensue, but they are guided by higher forces. Dorothy wears a pair of Ruby Red Shoes which possess magical power and she bears the protective kiss of the Good Witch on her forehead. As long as Dorothy listens to the right voice and stays focused on getting to Oz, she cannot fail.

The Tin Woodman's story is a wonderful tale of having been in love and wanting to be in love again. There is no blame. There is no guilt. There is no anger.

Chapter Three

If Only I Had a Heart

FARTHER DOWN THE YELLOW BRICK ROAD, Dorothy and the Scarecrow come upon something shiny positioned between the trees that stops them in their tracks. Upon further investigation they find a man made entirely of tin who stands perfectly motionless. Dorothy hears him make some sounds.

Baum wrote, "Did you groan?" she inquires.

"Yes," answers the Tin Woodman, "I did. I've been groaning for more than a year, and no one has ever heard me before or come to help me."

"What can I do for you?" she inquired, softly, for she was moved by the sad voice in which the man spoke.

"Get an oil can and oil my joints," he answered.

Dorothy and the Scarecrow look all around and then locate the oil can. They begin to carefully and methodically oil all the places in the Tin Woodman's body that are supposed to move and bend. Suddenly, the parts of him that have rusted and become immobile begin to move. When the Tin Woodman finds out that Dorothy and the Scarecrow are on their way to see the Wizard of Oz to ask for his help in getting back home and acquiring a brain, the Tin Woodman asks if he too can join them because he wants a heart.

In his novella, *The Little Prince*, Antoine de Saint Exupery reveals the secret of the fox, "Only the heart can rightly see." Having a heart gives us compassion and reverence for all living things. It gives us respect for the differences and the uniqueness of others and the ability to reach out to those in need. Having a heart enables us to live life richly and to enjoy the simple pleasures even if we aren't financially wealthy. It allows us to open our eyes and ears to the beauty and wonder that is all around us. Having a heart gives us the capacity to both give and receive love.

Dorothy and the Scarecrow give the Tin Woodman hope. Through the power of their belief that the Wizard of Oz is going to grant their wishes, he too becomes inspired and his imagination is awakened. As he looks down the yellow brick road he envisions something wonderful happening in the near future. He is appreciative that someone finally hears him, someone has taken notice, and someone has extended a hand to help mobilize him towards his life dream.

To help another in need is one of the greatest pleasures and most gratifying experiences life has to offer. People need to be carefully listened to, genuinely respected, and treated with kindness so they can become free from being stuck. If we pay attention, we will find people all around us who need a helping hand.

Mother Teresa made extending her hand and helping the poorest of the poor her life's work. Thousands of women and men were so inspired by both her message and her actions that they joined with her on her journey.

"Each one of us was created to love and be loved," she wrote. Mother Teresa was an exemplary living example of love in action.

Having good intentions is important but it is through action that things manifest. This action is two fold: it is the integrity of the mind harmoniously joined with the wisdom of the body. Mother Teresa had a marvelous mind and was a compelling speaker. But it was her caring actions and the power of love that flowed through her that inspired and drew thousands of women to her ministry.

Baum wrote, "The greatest loss I had known was the loss of my heart. While I was in love I was the happiest man on earth; but no one can love who has not a heart, and so I am resolved to ask Oz to give me one," said the Tin Woodman.

Tin Woodman is right. To love another is one of the greatest experiences in life and to be loved in return with equal passion is a miracle to be cherished. Love is essential to life. Love is life. Love shines as the subject of poets, the music of composers, and the lyrics of song writers. Once we are touched by the magic of love we are never quite the same. Once we taste the nectar of love we are not satisfied with anything less. Love transforms ordinary life into an extraordinary experience.

Each one of us has many stories to tell about love. Sometimes we spend more time recalling the tragic and disappointing memories of love rather than the memories of passion and joy. What we draw on from the past becomes what we manifest in the present and what unfolds in the future. What we focus on from the past sets the tone for what the future brings. The past is our reference point. The past holds our touchstones. Therefore, one of the healthiest ways to use the past is to recapture all of the highlights there. Highlights are the wonderful experiences, the memories that make us smile, the pictures that fill us with delight, the images and stories from our past that bring radiance to our faces.

Often, when we are hurt, we spend much of our time dwelling on what didn't work. We focus on the ways we were deceived, the mistakes we made, or how stupid we were. Hurtful experiences require time to heal. When we are emotionally reeling from a painful loss, the best thing for us to do is to 'just be' with the loss. Elizabeth Kubler Ross taught us that grief is a process and this process takes time. Therefore, when we experience a loss we need to give ourselves time to grieve.

Sometimes we get ahead of ourselves and think that we need to forgive and let go. Like grief, forgiveness takes time and we must respect our individual differences and time frames for the healing process to naturally run its course. Some of us heal quickly and some of us require years of reflection and inner work before we are able or willing to let go and move on.

No matter how long our healing takes, forgiveness is the last step. Without forgiveness, we will not be able to open our hearts again. As we forgive ourselves and others, we open the way for even deeper levels of intimacy. As we forgive, we open the way to inner peace. What we dwell on from the past is what we manifest in the present and in the future. Where we place our attention becomes what we tend to replicate in life again and again.

The Tin Woodman says that when he was in love, he was the happiest man on earth. Isn't that true for all of us? When we are in love we ARE the happiest people on earth. The Tin Woodman didn't say, "When I was in love I was the happiest person on earth and then that idiot left me. I will never forgive her or trust my heart to another again!" That story does not have a good ending. That story is the source of much suffering and disappointment in love today. When we continually think about the sad and sometimes tragic life experiences that seem to uncontrollably run through our minds, we shut down our hearts.

The Tin Woodman's story is a wonderful tale of having been in love and wanting to be in love again. There is no blame. There is no guilt. There is no anger. Because Dorothy hears his cry for help and extends her hand, the Tin Woodman's hope for loving and being loved is reawakened and his imagination is revitalized. The truth sets him free. Now, he excitedly moves toward his future goal: to get a heart and to love again.

The Tin Woodman could easily choose to stay stuck in that spot in the woods groaning but unwilling to respond when a hand is extended. He could decide that loving isn't worth the risk of a broken heart again. He could continue to review all the sad love tales from his life again and again reinforcing his belief that love is too dangerous to pursue. He could do a lot of things but he chooses to love again. He chooses the path with a heart.

In Carlos Castaneda's book, *The Teachings of Don Juan*, Castaneda poses the question, "Is there a way to avoid pain?" Don Juan responds, "Yes there is a way. Look at every path closely and deliberately. Try it as many times as you think necessary. Then ask yourself and yourself alone one question. Does this path have a heart? If it does, the path is good. If it doesn't it is of no use. One path makes you strong, the other weakens you."

Throughout Baum's story, Dorothy radiates a child-like innocence and love that transforms everything on her path as she makes her way to the Emerald City. She cares deeply about the welfare of others and her actions are inspired by generosity. She lives her life with integrity. As a result, Dorothy's love brings good things to her. She always magnetically attracts all the resources necessary to make the changes she needs to make and to get to where she needs to go. The power of her love and her compassion for every living thing instills within her a deep faith in life. Love, when given with an open heart, begets more love.

Glinda lovingly helped Dorothy begin her journey to Oz. When we need help, who do we turn to? There are more resources available to us today to help us learn to love again than at any time in history. An abundance of books, seminars, classes, support groups, counselors, TV shows, magazine and internet articles offering us information and assistance about love are right at our fingertips. Yet in spite of this, feelings of loneliness and depression are on the rise. Obesity, anxiety, and stress related illnesses are increasing. Drug use and alcoholism are growing. What aren't we learning and what are we failing to pay attention to?

We need look no further than to all the places inside us where we are holding feelings of disappointment, anger, resentment, guilt, and fear. These states of mind represent all that separate us from really loving and being loved. Our histories contain the seeds that grow into our present and future experiences of love. The inner places of anger are our walls. The memories of pain are our barriers. The inner places of fear are our defenses.

Like the Tin Woodman says, love asks that we open our hearts again and again. It asks that we let others off the hook, forgive, and let go of everything that disturbs our inner peace. Love invites us to be more accepting and caring toward ourselves and more accepting and caring toward others, that we do more of the things and say more of the words that bring us closer together. Love thrives on feelings of gratitude and is enhanced when we do the uplifting things that make us feel more alive. Love requires that we see others in all their glory: their beauty, grace, skills, abilities, gifts, wounds, darkness, and light. Love asks that we make the success of our intimate relationships a priority, that we take the time to learn the lessons of love, and that we acknowledge and embrace others for all that they are.

In the charming film, *Don Juan de Marco*, Johnny Depp, tells Marlon Brando that there are only four questions of value to ask:

"What is sacred?"

"Of what is the Spirit made?"

"What is worth living for?"

"What is worth dying for?"

Depp says, "The answer to each question is the same, LOVE!"

Dorothy, the Scarecrow, and the Tin Woodman are on a sacred path with a heart. It doesn't mean the path will be free of obstacles. Life is not free of obstacles and disappointments. Tragic things can happen despite our best intentions. But we must know and believe that we have the resources within and without to effectively respond to anything that life throws our way. Like Don Juan says in *The Teachings of Don Juan*, "Love makes us strong."

The path of love is an amazing journey. Some say that love is all there is. Love is the great healer. Love is why we are here. Love is transformative. To love and be loved is the greatest wisdom. No matter how one feels about love and sharing one's life with another, the only thing that holds us back from taking the risk again is fear. Fear creates obstacle after obstacle, leads to judgment and criticism, and prevents us from deeply and satisfy-ingly loving and being loved.

To love and be loved is life's most gratifying gift and greatest joy. And just as the Tin Woodman said, the happiest time in life is when we are in love.

Extraordinary people can and do enter your life just at the right time If you have the courage to pay attention. These remarkable people help you to find hope, love, and courage on your yellow brick road.

Chapter Four

If Only I
Had Courage

As Dorothy, the Tin Woodman, Toto, and the Scarecrow walk along the Yellow Brick Road, they begin to notice that the light is disappearing and they are entering a dark forest. They begin to pay more attention to the sounds of the wild, and fears begin to surface. Suddenly, a rowdy Lion appears and runs straight at them growling loudly. The three of them panic. The Lion swipes his paw at the Scarecrow who falls to the ground and then he takes a swipe at the Tin Woodman who topples over.

When the Lion goes after Toto, Dorothy quickly steps forward and slaps the Lion across the snout, scolding him for scaring her little dog!

Baum wrote, "Don't you dare to bite Toto! You ought to be ashamed of yourself, a big beast like you, to bite a poor little dog!"

"I didn't bite him," said the Lion, as he rubbed his nose with his paw where Dorothy had hit it. The Lion feels so humiliated that he begins to cry.

"You are nothing but a big coward. What makes you a coward?" asked Dorothy.

"It's a mystery," replied the Lion. "I suppose I was born that way."

"But that isn't right. The King of Beasts shouldn't be a coward," said the Scarecrow.

"I know it," returned the Lion, wiping a tear from his eye with the tip of his tail, "it is my great sorrow, and makes my life very unhappy. But whenever there is danger, my heart begins to beat fast."

Fear is a natural part of life. Awful things happen everywhere in the world and they are on full display twenty four hours a day on the internet and TV. If we buy into this news as the main focus of our reality, it follows that we would be filled with anxiety, despondency, and fear. Negativity promotes negativity. The Wicked Witch continually tries to frighten Dorothy by telling her that she is going to get her and her little dog too! This doesn't stop Dorothy from continuing on her journey to see the Wizard of Oz. She feels the fear, defies it, and moves on.

Like Dorothy, we can defy and transcend fear. Despite whatever fears we have, we can move forward and take the next steps toward our goals. We can stop seeing life myopically, instead see the bigger picture, and view life from a new and higher vantage point. We can hold the belief and vision that life is meant to be lived fully and passionately and not in the limited way fear dictates. We have lots of choices available to us when we confront and challenge fear.

The Lion asks the threesome where they are going. When they tell him, his mind is immediately filled with hope and his imagination comes alive.

"Can the Wizard of Oz give me courage?" he asks.

"I am sure the Wizard can give you some courage," responds Dorothy. "The Wizard will fix everything!"

Courage is a marvelous quality to possess. It takes courage to act even when we are uncertain of the outcome, courage to change, and courage to speak up for what we believe in. It takes courage to listen to the right voice and courage to remain confident even in difficult times and circumstances. It takes courage to stop being a victim and courage to remain true to who we are and to what we want to achieve. It certainly takes courage to face our hurtful feelings and it takes courage to love and be loved.

It takes courage to be creative. Everything we encounter that is man-made began as an image in someone's mind. Buildings, malls, bridges, homes, automobiles, books, art, films, furniture, computers, cell phones, music, video games, and thousands of inventions all first took form in the imagination. It takes courage to believe in our abilities, take what we see in the imagination, and shape it into something of value.

There are many books and teachings that stress the importance of living in the present moment, not venturing into the future or into the past, and recommending that we keep our focus in 'the now.' But this robs us of the richness of memory and imagination that can be harvested. *The Wizard of Oz* is an excellent example of how this is so. Dorothy doesn't want to stay with the Munchkins and the Good Witch of the North even though they want her to stay. She wants to go home. And off she goes, keeping her focus on the future and the excitement of getting back home to Kansas.

Her future focus keeps the momentum of the story moving forward in time. The mind has the remarkable ability to transcend time and 'the now' is just one point in an unlimited spectrum of time, a continuum that stretches forward and back.

There is something positively seductive and magical about playing with future possibilities that result in things of beauty. When Dorothy meets her three companions, the Scarecrow, the Tin Woodman, and the Lion, they too join her on the journey to Oz with the intention of getting something in the future that is extremely important to each of them. Using the mind and imagination to play in future time is one of the healthiest and most enjoyable things for us to do physiologically, psychologically, and spiritually.

When the painter and sculptor Michaelangelo was asked how he approached sculpting his masterpiece David, he replied that he chipped away everything in the large piece of marble that wasn't David! Michaelangelo had tremendous focus and concentration in present time, but if he hadn't also maintained his future vision of what David would look like, he would not have ended up with the incredible statue he envisioned. Our greatest hope is to learn from the past and to draw upon the wisdom there, to be fully absorbed in the present with focus, concentration, creativity, and joy, and to retain an inspiring vision of the future. Keeping these images alive in our minds and imaginations takes courage.

An excellent example of this is the story of the Russian composer and pianist, Sergei Rachmaninoff. The premier of his Symphony in 1897 in St. Petersburg, Russia met with such critical reviews by the local newspaper that Rachmaninoff fell into a depression for two years. Unable to recover from the trauma, he sought help from a physician by the name of Dr. Dahl, who specialized in auto-suggestion. Auto-suggestion is what self-hypnosis use to be called. During the two year period of his depression, Rachmaninoff was afraid to compose for fear of being ridiculed again. The critics had convinced him that his composition skills were worthless.

Dr. Dahl assessed Rachmaninoff's case and advised him to use the same hypnotic declaration day after day,

"I will start to compose a concerto. I will work with the greatest of ease. The composition will be of excellent quality!"

Even though this is a very elementary use of self-hypnosis, the affirmation worked for him. Rachmaninoff repeated these positive statements day after day for two years. During that time he began composing Piano Concerto No. 2. This composition had its world premier in October 1901. It was an instant success. Rachmaninoff's 2nd Piano Concerto is regarded one of the greatest piano concertos in classical music history. Not only did he rise to the occasion, he exceeded it. Dr. Dahl helped him to regain his confidence, let the past go, move beyond his fear, reignite the joy of composing, and to perform again in public.

Without a Dr. Dahl there may have not been Rachmaninoff's Piano Concerto No.2. Without the Good Witch Glinda, Dorothy may have not known what to do or where to turn for help. Without Dorothy, the Scarecrow would still be stuck on the pole. Extraordinary people can and do enter your life just at the right time IF you have the courage to pay attention. These remarkable people help you to find hope, love and courage on your yellow brick road.

When confronted about his needless attack on them, the Lion admits that he only attacks because he is afraid. In most cases, fear impels people to do things and say things that cause them and others problems, misunderstandings, and lots of regrets.

Dorothy, the Scarecrow, the Tin Woodman, and the Lion ultimately want to be healed, to return to a state of health and wholeness. Dorothy believes that she can only be healed by returning home, and she holds that image in her mind and imagination. The Scarecrow believes he can only be healed by acquiring a brain so that he can think, and he keeps that image alive. The Tin Woodman believes he can only be healed if he gets a heart so he can love again, and he holds that image in his mind and imagination. The Lion believes he can only be healed if he is given courage, and he lets the image of the Wizard bestowing this gift upon him propel him forward. And in their excitement about where they are going together, they join arm in arm, singing and skipping along the Yellow Brick Road, off to see the Wizard, the wonderful Wizard of Oz.

Obstacles strengthen Đorothy's resolve to get back home. They inspire the Scarecrow to use the brain he believes he doesn't have and they open the heart that the Tin Woodman fears he has lost. Obstacles open the door to the courage that the Lion worries he is missing. Overcoming obstacles helps them return to a state of grace.

Chapter Five

The Journey to the Wizard of Oz

"THEY HAD HARDLY BEEN WALKING AN hour when they saw before them a great ditch that crossed the road and divided the forest as far as they could see on either side. It was a very wide ditch, and when they crept up to the edge and looked into it they could see it was also very deep, and there were many big, jagged rocks at the bottom. The sides were so steep that none of them could climb down, and for a moment it seemed that their journey must end," wrote Baum.

Life tests our resolve again and again. Some things come easily to us and some things do not. Some goals are achieved with just a little effort and some goals require deep reserves of patience and determination. Some goals require the continued use of ingenuity, creative imagination, and outer and inner resources to make the dream a reality.

Dorothy, the Tin Woodman, the Scarecrow, and the Lion sit on the edge of the great ditch wondering what to do. One by one, each stands motionless trying to figure out what next step to take. It appears that they are stuck.

Baum wrote, "We cannot fly, that is certain; neither can we climb down into this great ditch. Therefore, if we cannot jump over it, we must stop where we are," said the Scarecrow.

"I think I could jump over it," said the Cowardly Lion, after measuring the distance carefully in his mind.

"Then we are all right," answered the Scarecrow, "for you can carry us all on your back, one at a time."

Confidently and courageously jumping and leaping over and over again, the Lion carries each of them one at a time. The Lion requires a bit of rest between each marvelous leap because this kind of exertion is unlike anything he has done before. Each leap with one of his companions on his back takes his breath away and he needs time to regain his strength and momentum to do it again.

Each time they go a little farther on their journey to Oz, they come up against another challenging obstacle. Every time this happens, one of them comes up with an idea that stirs their collective imagination and the obstacle is circumvented. The barriers inspire creative solutions, and solutions serve to strengthen their basic character and their resolve to succeed. As they walk along the yellow brick road they are developing the qualities they each believe they lack, growing in strength with each step they take towards the Emerald City.

The life of Walt Disney is a good example of coming up against barriers again and again and overcoming them. His teachers complained that he didn't pay attention to the instructions given for classroom assignments. Disney had an exceptionally vivid imagination and he was often scolded for adding human characteristics to plants and animals he was assigned to draw. He didn't let the teacher's words dissuade him and continually became more and more fascinated with the unlimited possibilities of drawing. Years later, animals and plants with human voices and attributes became the Disney trademark.

By the time he was seventeen, he had the ambition of becoming a cartoonist. By age twenty, Walt Disney was hired to draw cartoons for the Kansas City Film Ad Company. Within a short time he was making cartoons that moved, but they still didn't move the way that he had envisioned they could. He studied and worked tirelessly towards making a drawing move in more graceful and sophisticated ways so that it would have greater realism. These drawings and experiments took thousands of hours to perfect. When one approach failed, he tried another.

Walt Disney was the first person to sell the idea of having a cartoon open for a feature film. He sold cartoons by the linear foot to local movie theatres. Selling cartoons was not an easy thing. It required that he become a door to door salesman. Most theatre owners were not interested. But Disney was not put off. His focus, determination, and vivid imagination were his constant companions and it was these gifts that helped him get his cartoons into the theatres.

When he was twenty eight, he and his wife came up with the idea for a little character named Mickey Mouse. Theatre owners showed little interest in the mouse and he was unable to sell the clips. Again, he went to work. To make Mickey more enticing, Disney synchronized the mouse's movements to sound, making it the first cartoon of its kind. He named it Steamboat Willie. The year was 1927. Many theatre owners told him that the public would not be interested in cartoon characters and animals that talked.

He was convinced that Steamboat Willie was going to be a huge success at the box office and despite the poor response from vendors, Disney pressed on. He firmly believed in his product and strongly felt that film companies would eventually sign up for a series of Mickey Mouse cartoons. Steamboat Willie opened at theatres with great reviews and within a few years, Mickey Mouse became the most popular cartoon character in the country.

In 1937, Walt Disney released the first full movie version of a cartoon, *Snow White and the Seven Dwarfs*. This remarkable animated achievement required two million drawings. Most film makers thought Disney was nuts. Why would the general public sit and watch a full-length cartoon? Millions of adults and children swarmed into movie houses to see *Snow White and the Seven Dwarfs*. It was the success Disney envisioned it would be.

One of the most interesting things about Walt Disney is that he borrowed huge amounts of money to support the high cost of his animation work and film making. It was rumored that he was in debt millions of dollars for most of his adult life. He didn't consider cost a factor in making great films and he spent whatever it took to make his vision a reality. Lucky for him, his major benefactor was A.P. Giannini, the founder and board chairman of Bank of America. Even though Disney suffered many huge financial losses with Pinocchio, Fantasia, and other innovative films, Giannini continued to loan Disney money because he recognized his eccentric genius, his indomitable spirit, and his wildly creative imagination. He helped Disney use his mind, ingenuity, and heart to move ahead with courage. Without his help, Disney might not have been able to fully live his dream.

Similarly, Dorothy supports the Scarecrow, the Tin Woodman, and the Lion in achieving their dreams. Without Dorothy, each of them might easily remain just as she finds them. Dorothy is a catalyst for change and transformation. Like Disney, she is a dream maker.

Baum wrote, "Suddenly, Dorothy, the Scarecrow, the Tin Woodman, and the Lion came upon a broad river flowing swiftly just before them. On the other side of the water they could see the road of yellow brick running through a beautiful country, with green meadows dotted with bright flowers and the road bordered with trees hanging full of delicious fruits."

"How shall we cross the river?" asked Dorothy.

"That is easily done," replied the Scarecrow. "The Tin Woodman must build us a raft, so that we can float to the other side."

The Tin Woodman cuts down many small trees with his powerful axe and before they know it, they are floating across the river. Suddenly, they find themselves in a very strong current and their raft is being pushed farther and farther down river. With a burst of courage, the Lion jumps from the raft and swims with all of his might pulling the raft toward the shore as the Tin Woodman holds onto his tail. Once they reach the shore, they rest. The next day they awaken with renewed hope and inspiration. Like the animation work of Walt Disney, each obstacle they overcome brings them closer to their goal.

As they walk with the sight of the yellow brick road in the distance, they come upon a glorious meadow of poppies, the scent of which is so powerful, that anyone who breathes it for a prolonged period of time falls asleep. The Scarecrow and the Tin Woodman are unaffected, but Dorothy, Toto, and the Lion grow more tired by the minute and then fall into a deep sleep. In the film version, the poppy field is seen as a trap set up by the Wicked Witch, but in the book it is just one of many obstacles for them to overcome. Obstacles are a part of all myths, fables, stories, and dreams. A life without obstacles would be quite boring. They test our resolve. They test our patience. Obstacles help us to bring the power of the imagination into play.

Some obstacles, like the great ditch, seem overwhelming and too great to overcome. Some obstacles, like getting across the river, require the help and perspective of others. Some obstacles, like the Lion's cowardice, are self-created and self-inflicted. Some challenge us, like the Wicked Witch, helping us to face our fears. Some are just part of life. Without obstacles, we cannot tap into the best of whom and what we are. Challenges force us to use our heads, to open our hearts, to free our imaginations, and to let our inner courage come forth to 'test the waters' of change.

Just using the mind creatively and thinking about what we might do in a challenging situation is a good first step to being successful. Opening the heart is an essential second step, because without an open heart life is empty and unfulfilling. Opening the heart enlivens us and enriches our experiences. It is what gives relationships their depth and opens us to the inner world of feelings. Courage moves us forward and it helps us to take action. The imagination opens doors, helps us to see the bigger picture of where we are headed in life and what we are moving toward. Obstacles strengthen Dorothy's vision and tenacity. They inspire the Scarecrow to use the brain he thought he didn't have and they open the heart the Tin Woodman fears he has lost. Obstacles open the door to the courage the Lion worries he is missing. Overcoming obstacles helps each of them return to a state of grace.

Dorothy, Toto, and the Lion, unlike the Scarecrow and the Tin Woodman, are living flesh and require sleep to rejuvenate their bodies and spirits. Having been continually on the move day after day and meeting obstacles head on, they are more tired and weary than they realize. Once they close their eyes, they fall into a deep and restful sleep.

A few hours later, the Scarecrow and the Tin Woodman decide to wake up Dorothy, Toto, and the Lion and get them out of the poppy field. They are afraid that if they don't, they might never gain consciousness, or at the very least they might sleep for a very long time. Once their eyes are open, the four of them can once again see the yellow brick road in the distance. The vision of that road brings a smile to their faces and strengthens their determination to get to the Emerald City.

People hold and use their power in different ways. Some people hold power with intimidation. Some people acquire power as they accumulate wealth and material possessions. Some people gain positions of power through their remarkable gifts. Some people move into powerful leadership positions by touching the lives of others in amazing ways.

Chapter Six

Arriving at the Seat of Power

ONCE THEY SEE THE ASTOUNDING VISION of the Emerald City before them, their excitement can hardly be contained. They stop at the gate. Dorothy sees a bell, presses it, hears a twinkling sound, and the big gate slowly swings open. They pass through and find themselves in a highly arched room, the walls of which glisten with countless emeralds. The guard asks them what they want.

Baum wrote, "We are here to see the Great Oz!" said Dorothy.

"He is powerful and terrible and if you come for an idle or foolish errand, he might get angry and destroy you all in an instant!" said the guard.

"But it is not a foolish errand, nor an idle one," replied the Scarecrow; "it is important. And we have been told that Oz is a good Wizard."

The guard agrees to take them to Oz's palace, but first they must put on spectacles. The spectacles have green lenses in them and are fastened to the head in such a way that they cannot be removed. Spectacles must be worn by all within the palace grounds to make everything appear green. However, in the film, the Emerald City is simply green.

Anytime we wear colored glasses, the world looks different. When we see a 3-D film, we wear special glasses that give the illusion of the characters in the film popping out of the screen and standing right in front of us. Colored glasses change the reality of the outside world and the Grand Wizard wants to give the impression that the entire Emerald City is really green. This is one way he holds and wields his power.

The Wicked Witch wields her power through the stark black color of her clothes, the shrilling sound of her voice, the wickedness of her laugh, the intimidating way she moves, and the pageantry of her smoke-filled disappearance. The Good Witch Glinda embraces power in her beauty, in the kindness and gentleness of her manner, in the eloquence of her speech, in the queenly way she dresses, and in the grandeur of her smile.

People hold and use their power in different ways. Some people hold power with intimidation. Some people acquire power as they accumulate wealth and material possessions. Some people gain positions of power through their remarkable talents. Some people become powerful leaders by touching the lives of others in amazing ways.

Dorothy, the Scarecrow, the Tin Woodman, and the Lion are now at the seat of power. They are at the home of the Great Wizard of Oz and very close to meeting him. They have finally arrived at their destination. They hold the vision that they will be given what they came for and they believe that the Great Wizard has the power to bestow these gifts upon them.

One by one, they are allowed to stand before the Wizard and to ask him to grant their wish. He speaks to them in a frightening and thundering voice and uses many visual stunts to make him appear as though he can end their lives in the wink of an eye. Frightened and shaking, the four of them timidly press ahead with their requests.

Baum wrote, "I'll grant your wishes if you do something for me. You must kill the Wicked Witch of the West!" said the Wizard.

The four of them look at each other and realize that this is not going to be easy. Chopping down a tree or leaping over a ditch or building a raft are pieces of cake compared to what the Wizard is asking them to do. No one in their right mind wants to do battle with a powerful and Wicked Witch.

Baum wrote, "I suppose we must try it; but I am sure I do not want to kill anybody, even to see Aunt Em again," said Dorothy.

Dorothy will do just about anything to get back home, but she is unwilling to kill the Wicked Witch to accomplish that end. Taking another's life, no matter how evil that person may be, is not justified for any reason, Dorothy thinks.

The film script lightens their task a bit by asking them to bring back the Witch's broom. But Baum's original text is more specific and more demanding. The Wizard of Oz wants the Wicked Witch dead and he wants her dead for a very personal reason.

In her confrontation with the Wicked Witch, Dorothy discovers that she has the courage and power to stand toe to toe and face to face with the dark side of life and to win claim to what is rightfully hers.

Chapter Seven

The Battle with the Wicked Witch

As the four of them make their journey to find the Wicked Witch, they don't realize it, but she has already spotted them with her exceptionally keen eye sight. From far off in the distance she watches them as they make their way towards her territory. She immediately calls upon a great pack of wolves and instructs them to find Dorothy, the Scarecrow, the Tin Woodman, and the Lion and to tear them to pieces. But her evil and power cannot camouflage her fear. She knows that Dorothy wears the magic Ruby Red Shoes and has the kiss of protection on her forehead.

The Scarecrow and the Tin Woodman hear the wolves approaching.

"This is my fight," said the Tin Woodman; "so get behind me and I will meet them as they come," wrote Baum.

He grabs his mighty axe and with the heart of a warrior, one by one, The Tin Woodman chops off the heads of forty wolves.

The Wicked Witch is furious when she sees this happening. She immediately summons another attack. She calls upon wild crows to peck out their eyes and tear them to pieces. When Dorothy sees the wild crows approaching she becomes afraid.

"This is my battle!" says the Scarecrow. "Lie down beside me and you will not be harmed," wrote Baum.

The Scarecrow throws up his arms, yells wildly and scares the crows away. The ones he can't scare, he fights off with his hands. Again, the Wicked Witch is not able to harm them.

Next, she orders a swarm of black bees to attack them, but the Scarecrow is too clever. He tells Dorothy to pull his straw out and cover herself, Toto and the Lion with it, thus protecting them from the potential stinging of the bees. The bees find no one to sting except for the Tin Woodman. As they fly full force into him they are smashed against the tin.

Next, the Wicked Witch sends the Winkies to attack them. Once they approach, the Lion gathers all of his courage and springs forth with a great roar and frightens them away.

Finally, in her desperation, the Wicked Witch sends the Winged Monkeys to bring Dorothy back to the castle.

"We dare not harm this little girl," said the leader of the Winged Monkeys, "for she is protected by the Power of Good, and that is greater than the Power of Evil. All we can do is carry her to the castle of the Wicked Witch and leave her there," wrote Baum.

They experience one enormous challenge after another and somehow this surprisingly resilient foursome always comes through. Each conflict is successfully met with creative solutions. They face fear head on and they defy each clash with death. But the winged monkeys prove to be too powerful for them to overcome and they succumb, losing this final battle. As a result, the Scarecrow and the Tin Woodman are left behind and badly beaten, and the Lion is held captive in the courtyard of the Witch's castle.

Dorothy is brought directly to the Wicked Witch. She looks down at Dorothy's feet, sees the magic shoes, and begins to tremble with fear, for she knows that these shoes hold a powerful charm. But, the Wicked Witch also notices that Dorothy retains the naivety of a child and does not realize the power she has at her disposal. She decides to use Dorothy's innocence against her.

Baum wrote, "I can still make her my slave, for she does not know how to use her power," laughed the Wicked Witch.

Most of us do not know how powerful we really are and therefore often remain slaves to those who intimidate us. Coming into our power means coming to the realization that we are never helpless. We always have resources within us and around us that can assist and inspire us.

Despite this resourcefulness, some of us remain slaves to attitudes we learned from our parents. These beliefs can limit our happiness for an entire lifetime. Many of us remain slaves to values we learn from the media. Some of us remain slaves to beliefs and fears about love that prevent us from opening our hearts and really loving again. Some of us remain slaves to an unfulfilling life because we have never come to realize how creative we are. Some of us remain fearful because we are not conscious of the inner courage available to us for change.

Dorothy becomes the Wicked Witch's slave and through her intimidating voice and threats, she continues to keep Dorothy in a state of fear. This is exactly where she wants her to be; in a state of fear. But she wants more. She wants the power inherent in Dorothy's shoes so she can be the most powerful Witch in the land. She devises a plan to get them.

Resorting to trickery, the Wicked Witch makes a bar of iron and puts it in the middle of the kitchen. She then makes the bar invisible so that Dorothy will inadvertently trip over it. As planned, Dorothy stumbles over the metal bar and the Wicked Witch quickly grabs one of the magic shoes that falls off of Dorothy's foot. Now the Witch holds half the power and charm of the shoes. This infuriates Dorothy and she demands that the Wicked Witch give her back the shoe. The Witch not only refuses to give her back the shoe, but she laughs at Dorothy and tells her she is going to steal the other one too. In her frustration and anger, Dorothy picks up the closest thing to her, a bucket of water, and throws it on the Witch, drenching her from head to toe. Instantly the Witch gives out a loud cry; for she knows that in a few minutes she will melt away.

In her innocence, Dorothy has no idea that this will happen. She has no intention of harming the Witch. In that defining moment, Dorothy could choose to get into a physical battle with the Witch. She could grab something to strike her, but she has no desire to hurt her. Instead, she instinctively reaches for a bucket of water and drenches the Witch with it. Within seconds, the Wicked Witch is dead.

Dorothy's antagonistic relationship with the two Witches is nothing less than amazing. First, her house falls from the sky and lands on the Wicked Witch of the East killing her instantly. Serendipitously, Dorothy inherits her magical Ruby Red Shoes. Then, standing up for herself because the Wicked Witch of the West steals one of her shoes and won't give it back, Dorothy throws water on her and watches as she slowly melts into nothingness. As a result, Dorothy immediately takes her shoe back, regains her full power, and wins her freedom from bondage. Instinctively, she usurps the Witch's power by striking her where she is most vulnerable.

In the film version of the story, Dorothy throws water on the Witch because the Witch sets the Scarecrow on fire. In her effort to save the Scarecrow's life, Dorothy throws the water on him, but much of the water also lands on the Witch. The original story written by Baum makes more sense because anyone in the same situation would try to save their friend's life by throwing water on them. Baum, though, had a different intention in writing the scene in this way. It took bravery to directly confront the Wicked Witch and to throw a bucket of water on her. In doing this, Dorothy steps into her own power and wins her freedom.

We read so much about the power of intention and that setting an intention makes us magnetic for good things to come into our lives. Why, then, does Dorothy receive these tremendous gifts without setting an intention? Did L. Frank Baum not know about the power of intention when he wrote the Wizard of Oz?

The power of intention is a bit over blown in today's self help book market. What Baum depicts here are examples of serendipity. Serendipitous events represent the divine providence that appears to come our way quite by accident. But, this 'so called' accident is really the result of living a good life and being in a state of grace. Some might refer to these experiences as miracles. Love inspires miracles and love inspires serendipity.

Dorothy is a girl who lives life with an open and compassionate heart. Love guides her life. She is a girl with very strong integrity, conviction, and exemplary values. She extends her hand to help others wherever help is needed. She moves through life from the purity of her innocence and she deeply cares about the welfare of others. Dorothy has all the qualities that magnetically attract good things to her and the resources to assist her in meeting any challenge she is confronted with. She seems to always be in the right place at the right time. Thus, serendipity makes sense.

The great symbol of protectiveness and magic that appears from beginning to end in *The Wizard of Oz* is that of the Ruby Red Shoes. The shoes set the tone for the conflict between Dorothy and the Wicked Witch of the West right from the beginning of the story. The Wicked Witch is obsessed with getting those shoes. Because the shoes belonged to her sister (the Wicked Witch of the East) the Ruby Red Shoes become a constant source of antagonism between Dorothy and the Witch.

Dorothy begins her journey to Oz with the magical shoes on her feet, asserting her power step by step. It is a key element in the story that she does not realize how much power she has in her possession. She just embarks on her journey with an open heart, hope, protection, and the belief and vision that the Wizard of Oz is going to assist her in getting back home.

In many myths and stories, shoes are a symbol of power. They represent how solidly we stand on the ground and how well the earth supports us as we move on our journey. When Dorothy throws the water on the Wicked Witch, she 'puts her foot down.' Putting her foot down is an assertion of her power. But why would pouring water on the Wicked Witch cause her death? Why would something as simple as water have the capacity to melt the Witch?

Throughout literature and mythology, water has been depicted as the great symbol of transformation. Water represents the unconscious mind. Water holds the secrets of the ocean's depths. Water purifies. Water sustains life. The great Sages have said that if they had to choose to be just one element, they would choose water. Water always moves towards its source. It cannot be impeded in its determination to get to where it is headed. Water will flow under, around, over, and through to get to where it is going.

In this defining moment of the story, Dorothy instinctively grabs the resource that is closest to her and throws it on the Wicked Witch. The Witch has crossed over a precious boundary. She has taken something away from Dorothy that had been given to her by Glinda the Good Witch as a gift to guide her journey back home. Water is the most powerful element at her disposal and she instinctively uses it to win her freedom.

The Wicked Witch of the West threatens to rob Dorothy of the power and dignity that the magical shoes represent. The Witch can keep Dorothy imprisoned but cannot take away her thoughts, imagination, intuition, love, instincts, or courage to survive.

In his captivating book about his life as a prisoner in a concentration camp in Germany during World War Two, *Man's Search for Meaning*, Viktor Frankl wrote, "The prisoner who had lost faith in the future, his future, was doomed. With his loss in the belief in the future, he also lost his spiritual hold."

In her determination to survive, Dorothy destroys the Witch. In her determination to take back her shoe, and ultimately to get back home, Dorothy douses the Witch with water. She is not trying to destroy her. She simply wants what is rightfully hers and she draws upon her natural survival instincts. She listens to the right voice and refuses to let the Witch victimize her. Standing solidly in her power, Dorothy protects herself, and now she is free. Dorothy is free because everything she does is based upon values and inner qualities that spring from her heart.

Frankl continues, "A thought transfixed me: for the first time in my life I saw the truth as it is set to song by so many poets, proclaimed as the final wisdom by so many thinkers. The truth- that love is the highest goal to which man can aspire. Then I grasped the meaning of the greatest secret that human poetry and human thought and human belief have to impart: The salvation of man is through love and in love."

The true power players in the world do not know of the power they possess. What they do know is why they are here and what they are here to do. This kind of clarity helped Mother Teresa attract thousands of women and men and millions of dollars worth of property to assist her in her work with poverty. This clarity of vision helped Walt Disney attract the financial resources he needed to help him create one of the most innovative forms of entertainment ever conceived. What these two people had in common was a well-spring of passion for what they did. Passion is magnetic and its magnetism opened doors for them, availing them of more and more opportunities through which to express their vision and imagination in a variety of ways.

We could look at each of these people and conclude that the power of their intention was so strong that they attracted these wonderful gifts to themselves. Millions of people in the world have the power of intention to do something that makes them successful but it doesn't necessarily result in making the world a better place. Some people accumulate real estate, win fame, or amass wealth and *that* is the end of it, *that* is their goal! Bill and Melinda Gates are now using their wealth and power to do their philanthropic work in Africa. It is obvious they had an awakening, a calling to take billions upon billions of dollars and fund humanitarian projects in Africa for the poorest of the poor.

Many of us don't allow the feelings of love and kindness to be expressed fully in the things we do and in the goals we work towards. We don't use our heads or our great inquisitive minds enough to improve the conditions around us. We don't let the courage and compassion within us come alive to contribute to the health and well-being of others. Like Dorothy, we just want to go home and return to the false safety and familiarity there.

Dorothy's higher guidance is leading her in another direction. Before she can go home, she has to first go on a journey of the mind, the heart, and the imagination. As in many myths and legends, Dorothy has to bravely confront and successfully complete a variety of challenging and life-changing tasks as part of her initiation into the spiritual realm.

On her transformative journey to Oz, Dorothy discovers wonderful things about herself. She discovers that she is capable of drawing upon her compassion to help those in need. She realizes that she has a remarkable mind and imagination and can truly make a difference in the lives of others, a difference that results in fulfilling and lasting change. Most importantly, in her confrontation with the Wicked Witch, she learns that she has the courage and power to stand toe to toe and face to face with the dark side of life and to win claim to what is rightfully hers.

Dorothy is a girl with tremendous power that far exceeds the power of the Wizard of Oz. Her power is real because it arises from a place of integrity. The path of integrity beholds our greatest resources. When we are on this sacred path living our truth, nothing can really harm us. We might get delayed, make mistakes, or become overwhelmed with fear, but living in our truth will always take us back to our yellow brick road.

Chapter Eight

The Wizard Unveiled

AFTER DOROTHY WINS HER FREEDOM FROM the bondage of the Wicked Witch, she goes into the courtyard of the castle where the Lion has been held captive and tells him what has happened. She tells the Lion that she wants to find the Scarecrow and the Tin Woodman.

Baum wrote, "Do you suppose we could rescue them?" she asked.

"We can try," answered the Lion.

With the help of the Winkies, who she now commands, Dorothy and the Lion find the Tin Woodman and the Scarecrow. Both have been badly beaten. The Scarecrow's arms and legs have been pulled apart and the straw which made up his inner body lies scattered about. The Tin Woodman is not in any better shape. His tin is smashed and severely dented and he too is in need of repair.

The Winkies pick them both up and carry them to the castle for renovation. Once there, Dorothy has the Scarecrow stuffed with new straw and then she stitches all the seams. Within a short time he is as good as new. The Tin Woodman needs his tin to be hammered out and repaired by local tinsmiths. Then he too is as good as ever.

Now that the four of them are reunited again under very different circumstances, they rejoice at their new found freedom and position.

Baum wrote, "We must go back to Oz and claim his promise," exclaimed Dorothy.

"Yes," said the Tin Woodman, "at last I shall have my heart."

"And I shall get my brains," added the Scarecrow joyfully.

"And I shall get my courage," said the Lion thoughtfully.

"And I shall get back to Kansas," cried Dorothy, clapping her hands. "Let us start for the Emerald City tomorrow!"

After a long journey, Dorothy, the Scarecrow, the Tin Woodman, and the Lion approach the gates to the Emerald City and ask for admittance. The guard is surprised to see them there again. When he finds out that Dorothy has melted the Wicked Witch, he excitedly opens the gate. Word quickly spreads throughout the Palace of Oz that Dorothy has killed the Witch and a huge crowd begins to form.

The next day, the four of them meet with the Wizard once again.

Baum wrote, "We have come to claim our promise," said Dorothy.

"What promise?" asked Oz.

"You promised to send me back to Kansas when the Wicked Witch was destroyed," said the girl.

"And you promised to give me brains," said the Scarecrow.

"And you promised to give me a heart," said the Tin Woodman.

"And you promised to give me courage," said the Cowardly Lion.

"Is the Wicked Witch really destroyed?" asked Oz.

"Yes," she answered. "I melted her with a bucket of water."

"Come to me tomorrow, for I must have time to think it over," replied Oz.

This makes the four of them furious and they demand that the Wizard be good for his promises! The Lion is so angry and roars so loudly, that Toto jumps away and tips over the screen that stands in the corner, revealing a little, old man, with a bald head and wrinkled face. He looks at the four of them in embarrassment. The Tin Woodman rushes toward him with his axe raised.

Baum wrote, "Who are you?" asked the Tin Woodman.

"I am Oz the Great and Terrible," said the little man in a trembling voice, "but don't strike me, please don't, I'll do anything you want me to."

The four of them stand there in shock, looking at the quivering face of this old and wrinkled man who they think is a great Wizard. He is not. Each of them demands exactly what he or she has traveled many days to receive. The Wizard has no choice but to grant their wishes; for no one has ever uncovered that he is an imposter. During his reign as Wizard, no one has ever questioned his authority.

The Wizard removes the Scarecrow's head, takes it into the back room, and fills it with bran, pins, and needles. He stuffs straw into all the empty spaces to give it a full look and then stitches the head back onto the Scarecrow's body telling him that he now has brains. The Scarecrow graciously thanks him and goes on his way.

Then the Wizard cuts a hole in the Tin Woodman's breast and places a beautiful sawdust stuffed silk heart inside it. He then replaces the square of tin and solders it into place. The Tin Woodman is very pleased.

Baum wrote, "Is it a kind heart?" asked the Tin Woodman.

"Oh, very!" answered the Wizard.

The Tin Woodman fully believes and accepts what the Wizard tells him and excitedly goes on his way.

Next, the Wizard pours some green liquid into a bowl and tells the Lion to drink it. He tells the Lion that in doing this, he will gain courage. Slowly, the Lion drinks the green liquid. The Wizard assures him that he is now full of courage.

Baum wrote, "How do you feel now?" asked the Wizard.

"Full of courage," replied the Lion.

All of these are examples of the power of suggestion. The power of suggestion is a remarkable force. It is so influential that negative suggestions can instill fear and take away our vitality. Positive suggestions can awaken optimism and help us to feel more alive.

The fact is, nothing is actually different and yet each of the characters believes that they have received what they assumed they were lacking. In science and medicine, this is called the placebo effect. In the field of Hypnosis, this is simply regarded as the power of the mind to fully accept a suggestion and effect change. The change occurs because there is no resistance to the suggestion offered.

Baum wrote, "It was easy to make the Scarecrow and the Lion and the Tin Woodman happy, because they imagined I could do anything. But, it will take more than imagination to carry Dorothy back to Kansas, and I am sure I don't know how it can be done," the Wizard mused.

Who, then, is the Wizard of Oz? He is a very simple man whose hot air balloon one day goes off course and comes down in the Land of Oz. Mesmerized, the natives of Oz watch him descend from the clouds and conclude he is a great Wizard. He immediately recognizes that they mistakenly believe he is a man of exceptional power, even though he is quite ordinary. He decides to use the power of their belief to his advantage and orders them to build the Emerald City. For dozens of years he uses trickery to keep this incredible secret from them and from the four Witches as well.

Oz is a gifted ventriloquist who can use his voice in convincing ways. He keeps the natives of Oz enslaved because they think he has the power to harm them and to take away their lives in the wink of an eye. His lies, antics, and trickery keep them in a state of fear.

Fear wears many disguises. Fear impels the citizens of Oz to follow the Wizard's orders. Fear keeps the four Witches at bay. Fear keeps the Scarecrow stuck on a pole. Fear keeps the Tin Woodman rusted and immobilized. Fear keeps the Lion confined to a very small space in the jungle. Fear prevents the Wizard of Oz from telling the truth.

But then, Dorothy comes along and changes everything. The Scarecrow gets brains and is freed, the Tin Woodman regains movement and gets a heart, the Lion expands his space and manifests courage, the Wicked Witches are abolished, and the Wizard of Oz is exposed for what he really is. She turns things around for the better. Her vision and determination to get back home to Kansas destroys evil, defies fear, and returns the Land of Oz back to its original state of benevolence and innocence.

Dorothy is a girl with tremendous power that far exceeds the might of the Wizard of Oz. Her power is real because it arises from a place of integrity. The path of integrity beholds our greatest resources. When we are on this sacred path and are living our truth, nothing can really harm us. We might get delayed, make mistakes, and temporarily become immobilized with fear, but living in our truth will always take us back to our yellow brick road. Once we are solidly on the path with yellow bricks, it will lead us to our highest and most fulfilling aspirations.

This is not an easy journey. It is complicated by one obstacle after another. But Dorothy, the Scarecrow, the Tin Woodman, and the Lion face each obstacle thoughtfully and courageously and eventually find their way to the Good Witch's castle.

Chapter Nine

The Journey Back Home

WITHIN A SHORT TIME, THE WIZARD comes up with the idea of making a hot air balloon to bring Dorothy back to Kansas. Together, the two of them cut and sew strips of silk, and within a few days, the hot air balloon is complete. Oz appoints the Scarecrow 'Ruler of Emerald City' and a big celebration is planned on the day the hot air balloon is to be launched.

Because she is looking for Toto, Dorothy is a few seconds late for take-off and the Wizard is lifted into the sky without her. Watching him fly away, Dorothy is momentarily devastated and thinks she will be stuck in the Emerald City forever. Fortunately, within minutes, she is told that the Good Witch might be able to help her get back home. The four of them slowly make their way to the Quadlings where the Good Witch of the South lives.

This is not an easy journey. It is complicated by one obstacle after another. But Dorothy, the Scarecrow, the Tin Woodman, and the Lion face each obstacle thoughtfully and courageously and eventually find their way to the Good Witch's castle.

In the film version, Glinda is the Good Witch who greets Dorothy at the beginning of the film and again at the end. But in Baum's original story, an old and Good Witch of the North greets Dorothy at the beginning of the story and Glinda the Good Witch of the South helps her at the end.

Once they arrive at Glinda's Castle, the four of them meet with her and discover she is a most kind and loving Witch. She tells Dorothy that she has always had the power to get back home anytime she wanted to because of the charm attached to her Ruby Red Shoes.

Baum wrote, "The Shoes," said the Good Witch, "have wonderful powers. And one of the most curious things about them is that they can carry you to any place in the world in three steps, and each step will be made with a wink of the eye. All you have to do is to knock the heels together three times and command the shoes to carry you wherever you wish to go."

Dorothy hugs and kisses her three friends goodbye. She clicks the heels of her shoes together three times, saying, "Take me home to Aunt Em!"

Suddenly, she finds herself spinning and whirling through the air, much like she had at the beginning of the story. Within a very short time, she is sitting on the broad Kansas prairie looking at the new farm house Uncle Henry has built. Aunt Em is watering the flowers when she sees Dorothy running towards her.

Baum writes, "My darling child!" she cried, folding the little girl in her arms and covering her face with kisses; "where in the world did you come from?"

"From the land of Oz," said Dorothy. "And here is Toto, too. And oh, Aunt Em! I'm so glad to be home again!"

It is our task, our spiritual work to slowly transform all the negative qualities associated with home and to turn them into positive qualities. If we identify the word 'unavailable' with our childhood memories, it is our task to spend time with people who are emotionally available to us. If we identify with the word 'hurtful,' it is our task to spend time with supportive and loving people. We must take the best of our childhood home life and replicate that! We must take the worst of our childhood home life and make it our life's work to not repeat it! Like Dorothy facing challenges on the yellow brick road with the help from the Scarecrow, the Tin Woodman, and the Lion, our spiritual work requires help from others. We are not alone.

Chapter Ten

Home Again

In the film version of *The Wizard of Oz*, Dorothy awakens from a dream surrounded by the farm hands, her uncle, and her aunt. Baum did not write this scene in his book because it was his intent that Dorothy really be taken on an unexpected journey to a magical place far, far away and successfully find her way back home. Hollywood portrayed it as a dream. Having worked with dreams professionally my entire adult life, I appreciate both endings, but I prefer Baum's.

Looking closely at the film and the book, the single theme both pose again and again is the significance of home. When Dorothy is home she dreams about being someplace else, and when she is someplace else she dreams about being back home in Kansas. While in Oz, her feelings about home are dramatically changed and her thoughts about home significantly shift. What home means to her in the past and what home becomes in her imagined future are both radically and positively altered.

No matter whom she meets, no matter what wonderful qualities they possess, no matter how beautiful Oz is, how much she is appreciated there, or what honors those she meets want to bestow upon her, Dorothy wants to go back home! The wonderful thing about her going back home is that she is returning a transformed girl. She is returning home self-confident, compassionate, and empowered. She has faced hardship and passed the test. She has faced adversity and found her footing. She has confronted death and risen up stronger than ever.

In the last few pages of Baum's book, when Dorothy is told to click her heels together three times and say where she wants the magical shoes to take her, she says, "Take me home to Aunt Em."

Hollywood has her saying, "There is no place like home."

There is a big difference here. *There is no place like home* has no punch to it. It is not the statement of a girl who has just experienced what Dorothy has experienced. In Baum's original story, Dorothy returns home a very confident child and her declaration in that moment would reflect that confidence.

If there is no place like home, what does your childhood home represent to you? This is a very important question, perhaps one of the most important questions you will ever ask yourself. The information gathered by asking this simple question may give important insights that will put your current life situations into perspective.

As an exercise, draw a circle the size of a silver dollar in the middle of a piece of paper and put the word HOME in the middle of the circle. Attach 10–12 lines from the edges of circle radiating out from it like the rays of the sun. On the tips of these rays, write the words you associate with your childhood home. You will end up with words and images like: nurturing, welcoming, frightening, safe, loving, noisy, scary, unavailable parents, peace, angry, deceptive, comforting, etc. Look at the words and notice how many of these words play an active part in your love life, your work life, and in your life in general.

It is our task, our spiritual work to slowly transform all the negative qualities associated with home and to turn them into positive qualities. If the word 'unavailable' appears in the circle, it is our task to use our heads and be more discriminating of the people we hang out with, making sure they are emotionally available to us and emotionally healthy for us. If the word 'hurtful' appears, it is our task to make wiser choices in spending time with supportive and loving people. We can take the best of our childhood home life and replicate it! We can take the worst of our childhood home life and make it our life's work to not repeat it, to change it, and do something more fulfilling! Like Dorothy facing challenges on the yellow brick road with the help from the Scarecrow, the Tin Woodman, and the Lion, our spiritual work requires help from others. We are not alone.

One of the key lessons Baum taught us in *The Wonderful Wizard of Oz* is to be open to receiving from each other. People can offer their help but unless we take it in, unless we accept the support and care extended, it will not change the course of our lives. Another lesson is that we are not alone. The Scarecrow, the Tin Woodman, and the Lion accepted the help offered to them by Dorothy. There are people close at hand that can help us get to where we want to go. We just need to pay attention, be open to receiving, and accept their assistance.

In a much broader sense, we may find that the words we associate with home are the same words we associate with love and intimacy; these are the same words we associate with the optimism or negativity with which we approach life; these are the same words we associate with God or a Higher Power. In short, our home of origin is a powerful player in setting the tone for all life's experiences. Freud was correct on this point. One of the many places he failed was in stating that our past determines our future. Our past impacts our future but does not necessarily determine it. We can change. We can make healthier choices. We can move beyond our childhood memories, traumas, and challenges. We have that freedom!

This is not an exercise to use to blame your parents, or to blame the past, or to blame anything or anyone for what you and your life have become. What was given to you is one thing. What you do with what was given to you is something else. God gave you your life. How you use your miraculous brain, your amazing imagination, your magnificent heart, and your courage is up to you. This is simply an exercise to help you gain insights into the possible origin influencing how you live life today, how deeply you love and let love in, and how much satisfaction or dissatisfaction you experience. The pulse and spirit of your childhood home impacts all of these.

When I read about the life of John Muir, the great environmentalist, I thought he must have had parents who took him into the woods on a regular basis and taught him about the wonders of nature.

What I discovered was shocking. John Muir's father, who was a minister, beat him daily with a belt to make certain that he kept his focus on bible studies. Muir tells story after story of his agonizing memories of lashings by his father.

Everyday, John Muir sought out the solace of Mother Nature to soothe his wounds and rekindle his spirit. Despite whatever hardship his father created for him, John Muir dramatically altered his childhood memories by becoming one with the spirit of nature. He often said that he found God in the beauty of nature. Instead of focusing on the strictness and unnecessary physical abuse he suffered at the hands of his father, Muir put all of his energy into discovering the wonders of nature and becoming a protector of these incredible natural resources. His father failed at protecting him so Muir turned this around and became a protector of the environment. Instead of holding on to painful memories and the unfair treatment he received at home, Mother Nature became his home. John Muir founded the Sierra Club and is responsible for the preservation of millions of acres of forests, mountains, rivers, and land. He helped establish Yosemite National Park, the preservation of the Grand Canyon, and the protection of other natural wonders. He is the author of twelve books and is regarded as the Patron Saint of the American Wilderness.

*It is important to fill our lives with
the imagery of up beat and inspiring
stories. Positive stories transport us into
an altered state of consciousness, instill
a feeling of harmony within us, and
offer us hope for the future. Uplifting
stories are resources that motivate us
again and again.*

Chapter Eleven

Tell Me a Story

STORIES ARE TRANCE-INDUCING. MANY WRITERS ARE masters at telling stories. Many public speakers have a gift for the art of telling stories because of the dramatic and entertaining way they speak. Perhaps our parents or grandparents were talented story tellers. Telling stories to impart wisdom and mastery is an art form in many cultures and tribes. Talented film makers, like those who made *The Wizard of Oz*, tell wonderful stories.

Some of us get caught up telling tragic stories from the past and sad stories from our childhoods. Some of us have very rigid story themes that focus on loss, illness, and fighting through adversity. But no matter what stories dominate our minds and imaginations, there is a great power inherent in sharing stories.

If the Scarecrow had told the story over and over again about not having a brain AND he had never been gifted one by the Wizard, then *The Wizard of OZ* would be a tragedy. If Dorothy had remained lost and had never found her way back home and had never met the Good Witch, had never felt protected, and had never met her friends who joined her in the journey to Oz, then her story would also be a tragedy.

Like a book or a film, if you view your life as a story in which you see things through the eyes of the lead actor, director, supporting cast, cinematographer, editor, and critic, it might put things into a clearer perspective.

As lead actor am I making changes, going on refreshing journeys, dealing with and overcoming conflict, and meeting wise people who guide me along the way?

Am I stuck in a rut doing the same unfulfilling things over and over again and repeating the same lines?

As lead actor, is my life very predicable or is it unpredictable?

Am I spontaneous or have I lost my spontaneity?

Is my film dark and depressing often or am I able to rise up above the difficulties and challenges using my imagination, ingenuity, and playfulness?

As director, how shall I direct the lead actor to make his or her role come alive?

What guidance can I give the lead actor to help him or her effect positive change?

What does the lead actor need to do to make his or her life a lot more interesting?

More passionate?

More Healthy?

More successful?

Are **my support characters** helping me on my journey or taking me farther away from my goal?

Am I learning important lessons from them or are they a negative influence?

Are my support characters fun to be with?

Do my support characters and I help each other in important ways?

Are my support characters helping me to grow spiritually?

Are they keeping me stuck?

As cinematographer, which scenes from my life are most memorable?

Which lengthy scenes would I like to shorten and which scenes would I like to elongate?

Which current scenes make me smile just to think about?

Which scenes would I call highlights?

Which scenes make me sad to think about?

As editor, what scenes and dialogue need to be deleted because they don't move the story and the lead character forward?

Which scenes from my past would I like to add back in?

Which scenes would I never put into my life film again?

Which words or actions does my inner editor stop that want to be expressed?

As critic, if I wrote two paragraphs about my current life, what would I write?

What aspects of my current life story are boring?

What sub-plots of my current life story make me feel alive?

Which ones deaden me?

Where in my story do I appear to be stuck?

In what chapters or scenes am I not making any progress?

In what chapters or scenes am I making a great deal of progress?

Which scenes am I excited about?

Which ones are fulfilling?

Which ones am I sick and tired of watching over and over again?

Which scenes or chapters am I ready to change so that the lead actor, ME, can move forward towards a goal that is important to my continued health and well being?

A story told from the heart, passionately acted, intelligently directed, and beautifully photographed poignantly touches us and opens our eyes and hearts.

In the last scene of the Academy Award winning film *Cinema Paradiso,* Toto (interestingly bearing the same name as Dorothy's little dog) watches the film clips left to him by Alfredo. Scene after scene, Toto is immersed in watching clips of lovers tenderly and passionately kissing that were deleted from films that were shown at his church many years ago. He is overwhelmed with emotion.

In the final scene of the Academy Award winning film *Ordinary People,* Donald Sutherland and Timothy Hutton, father and son, tell each other how much they love one another. They look into each others tear-filled eyes and lovingly embrace as Johann Pachelbel's hauntingly beautiful Canon in the key of D plays in the background.

A magical scene in *Somewhere in Time* shows Christopher Reeve being magnetically drawn to the photograph of Jane Seymour on the wall in a hotel museum. Once she holds his gaze, he is hypnotized by her angelic face. He travels on an amazing journey back in time to be with her again.

Great films depict hundreds of magical stories within a story. If we let our imaginations roam freely, we could probably tell dozens of stories using Dorothy's Ruby Red Shoes as a jump-off point

It is important to fill our life with the imagery of up beat and inspiring stories. Positive stories transport us into an altered state of consciousness, instill feelings of harmony within us, and offer us hope for the future. Uplifting stories like *The Wizard of Oz* are resources that motivate us again and again.

Look at each scene below which is either from the film, *The Wizard of Oz* or from Baum's book, *The Wonderful Wizard of Oz* and let your mind and imagination create a story. It can be a story from your past or a story that you create about the future. It can be a story you make up in the inner world of your imagination. It can be a story you tell or a story you write seen through the eyes of each of the main characters in *The Wizard of Oz*.

Seeing through the Eyes of Dorothy:

1. When the Wicked Witch refuses to return Dorothy's shoe, Dorothy throws a bucket of water on her. Tell a story about standing up for yourself as you face adversity or fear.

2. Glinda the Good Witch helps give Dorothy resources to assist her on her journey to Oz. Tell a story about a powerful person who

gave you encouragement and the resources to help you make your journey to the next phase of your life.

3. Glinda the Good Witch gives Dorothy a protective kiss. Tell a story about something someone gave you that helped you to feel safe and protected.

4. Before returning home, Dorothy tells the Scarecrow that she will miss him most of all. Tell a story about a special friend you will never forget.

5. Dorothy surrenders to the power of the cyclone and she surrenders to the power of the Wicked Witch. Both situations end very positively for her. Tell a story about the power of surrender.

6. During her journey inside of the cyclone, Dorothy remains calm and has the faith that things will work out OK. Tell a story about a time in your life you kept your poise and got through a difficult experience.

7. Dorothy's journey to Oz is magical. Tell a story about magical time in your life.

8. Dorothy sees the Scarecrow stuck on the pole and helps him down. She sees the Tin Woodman rusted and unable to move and oils his joints. Tell a story about the transforming power of service and helping others in great need.

9. Dorothy gives the Scarecrow, the Tin Woodman, and the Lion hope. Tell a story about a time in your life when someone inspired hope.

10. In the opening scenes of The Wizard of Oz, Dorothy sings the beautiful song, *Somewhere Over the Rainbow*. Tell a story about a place you

have dreamed or fantasized that is somewhere over the rainbow.

11. In the film version of *The Wizard of Oz*, Dorothy is awakened from her dream of traveling to Oz. Tell a story about an amazing dream you had. What does the symbolism of this dream mean to you? What guidance is this dream attempting to give to you in your current life story?

12. When in the company of the Good Witch Glinda, Dorothy asked for help to get back home. The Good Witch told her that perhaps the Wizard of Oz could help her with her request. Who do you go to when you need help?

13. Dorothy was continually pursued by a Witch who was trying to take her magical shoes away and subsequently seize the power they gave her. Is there someone or something in your current life that you believe is trying to take your power away from you? What are you doing to bring resolution to this situation?

14. In the film version of *The Wizard of Oz*, Dorothy clicks the heels of her magic Ruby Red Shoes three times repeating the words, "There's no place like home." Tell a story about clicking your heels together three times. Where do your magic shoes take you?

15. Dorothy had wonderful attributes that began to unfold as she made her way to Oz. Describe at least 5 attributes that you think best describes Dorothy. Which ones do you possess? Which ones would you like to work towards having?

16. The Scarecrow, the Tin Woodman, and the Lion all instinctively trusted Dorothy. What was it about her that would lead to instant trust? What is it about a person that allows you to instinctively trust them?

Seeing through the Eyes of the Scarecrow:

1. The Scarecrow was stuck on a pole. Tell a story about being stuck at some point in life only to be freed by using determination, wits, courage, and imagination.

2. The Scarecrow held beliefs about himself that limited him. What beliefs do you continue to accept and let run your life that you know no longer serve you?

3. The Scarecrow wanted a brain. What were some of the things you learned from the Scarecrow about having a brain?

4. Once off the pole, the Scarecrow felt a deep sense of hope about finally getting something that was very important to him. How would your life be different if you began living your life with greater hope and faith?

Seeing through the Eyes of the Tin Woodman:

1. The Tin Woodman describes the time he was in love as the happiest time in his life. Tell a

story about one of the happiest and most loving times in your life.

2. The Tin Woodman wanted a heart so he could love again. What were some of the important things you learned about love from the Tin Woodman?

3. The Tin Woodman wanted to love again. Tell a story about taking a risk at love again.

4. If you really expressed your love more in every day life, what would you be doing differently?

*Seeing through the Eyes of
the Lion:*

1. The Lion discovers that he really does have courage. Tell a story about discovering the power of courage.

2. Once you feel more trusting, courage and risk taking naturally follow. What did you learn from the Lion about courage?

3. If you had more courage, describe some of the brave acts you would engage in?

4. The Lion believed he was a coward and lived life fearfully. What single belief do you have currently that is holding you back from taking a risk in doing something you want to do?

5. Because he was afraid, the Lion spent his life in a very small space. If you could expand the scope of your life tomorrow and there was nothing stopping you, tell a story about your

new life, where you live, what you do, and how you spend your time.

Seeing through the Eyes of the
Four of Them:

1. Dorothy, the Scarecrow, the Lion and the Tin Woodman each successfully receive the gift they want. Tell a story about a special gift you want to receive.

2. When faced with challenges Dorothy, the Scarecrow, the Tin Woodman, and the Lion were able to bring creative solutions into play. Describe a problem or challenge you currently have and then brain storm with the help of three other people to help resolve it.

3. Dorothy, the Scarecrow, the Tin Woodman, and Lion became good friends on their journey to Oz. As you think about all the people you have known, which three friends would you take with you to Oz? Why?

4. Dorothy, the Scarecrow, Tin Woodman and the Lion were all deceived by the power of the Wizard of Oz. Despite this, they regained their focus and received the gifts they came for. Despite whatever setbacks you have suffered in your life, what gift do you still dream of receiving?

5. *The Wizard of Oz* is a story about self-empowerment, self-confidence, courage, inspiration, giving, love, and creatively using

the mind and imagination. Describe what you would do and how your life would be different if you woke up tomorrow with these qualities and had them for one full day?

6. *The Wizard of Oz* is filled with the music of fabulous songs, graceful movements, and energetic dances. The story is a testimony to the beauty of communicating in loving, respectful, and compassionate ways. This kind of loving and respectful communication brings the imagination to life. Tell a story about your imagination.

7. Dorothy, the Scarecrow, the Tin Woodman, and the Lion are very excited about their journey to Oz, a place they have never been before. Tell a story about the excitement of taking a journey to a place you have never been before.

8. When they arrive at the great ditch, Dorothy, the Scarecrow, the Tin Woodman, and the Lion first think they have come to the end of their journey. Using their wits and courage, they get across the wide ditch and continue on their way to Oz. Tell a story about coming up against a huge barrier and overcoming it.

Time travel can be a life changing journey. Where the mind goes, what it entertains, and how long it stays there, are vastly important to our present health and well-being and to the future we want to create. Paying attention to the places the mind travels to and learning to retrain it in the sojourns it takes is a valuable skill.

Chapter Twelve

Traveling Through Time in Your Mind and Imagination

When Dorothy removes the Scarecrow from the pole, he tells her that he wants a brain. Metaphorically, he is stuck in a particular life script, life pattern, and getting a brain means a lot more than just having the ability to think. It means having the capacity to dream uplifting dreams, having the aptitude to problem solve, having the talent to use the mind creatively, having the faculty to communicate in positive ways, having the skill to lovingly connect with another person, and having the gift to time travel using the imagination for enjoyment and self-discovery.

Each time Dorothy says, "I want to go back home to Kansas," she is traveling back in time in her mind as she recalls the memory of home. Instantaneously, she travels forward in time and sees herself arriving safely there. The mind and imagination work this quickly. In a millisecond, you can move back and forth in time in your mind and imagination.

When we look at photographs, the visual image automatically takes us back in time. A photograph can have a thousand words associated with it, numerous stories, and bring up dozens of other memories. When we think about things we have done, places we have traveled to, relationships we have had, or jobs we have held, we are on a sojourn in time. The imagery and related feelings can seem so real, it is like we are there again in present time.

Revisiting the past is a naturally occurring phenomenon that happens over and over again in the course of a single day. Simple conversations about what we did or where we went immediately take us back in time. Our life is filled with symbols from the past and these symbols stir up memories. A blanket, a painting, a film, a restaurant, a wine glass, a special book, or a certain street can immediately reconnect us with past memories. Just listening to the hypnotic lyrics of a song can transport us back in time to the emotionally charged images of a former lover.

Traveling back in time to memories can be a delightful endeavor or a miserable journey, depending upon what we are thinking about. We can recall and entertain images and memories that make us cry and feel depressed and we can entertain images and memories that make us laugh and feel good. If we use this skill *primarily* to think back in time to all of the things that didn't work out as we had hoped: divorces, separations, losses, disappointments, resentments, traumas and the like, then we are using the power of the mind to revisit situations that are painful and potentially unhealthy. Some of us have an addiction to recalling unhappy and unfulfilling memories that result in feelings of depression.

Recalling past memories over and over again that serve no positive or constructive purpose thwart creativity and severely narrow future possibilities for fun and enjoyment. If the stories we tell to our friends and family members are typically dark and make us feel sad and lonely, then we are stuck in mind travels that create hopelessness and limitation.

How do we get stuck? We get stuck in gloomy and murky places in our memories that no longer serve a helpful purpose. We get stuck in old and worn out recollections and stories. We get stuck in past chapters that bear no resemblance to what we are desperately seeking now and desire in the future. We get stuck because we have forgotten about the inherent power of our imaginations.

I heard a story about a man who, when crossing the border between Canada and the USA, was asked by the border patrolman, "Where have you been, how long have you been there, and where are you going?"

Upon hearing these three questions, the man had a kinesthetic response and immediately went into a trance. He thought these were three of the most profound questions he had heard in a long time. His mind and imagination were stirred as he sat motionless in his car, repeating the questions over and over again trying to capture their full significance.

Annoyed, the border patrolman knocked on his window trying to awaken the man from his trance. "Sir, please answer the questions. There is a long line of cars here."

It takes courage to answer these three questions honestly. Our answers reveal whether we see our past in a grand way or in a limited way and what we hope to embrace in the future.

Where have I been?

How long have I been there?

Where am I going?

If you find the answers to these three questions pleasing and the images they bring up make you smile, then your past supports you, and your imagination will serve you well. If you find that the answers to these three questions sadden you and your face becomes sullen, then your past needs to be reexamined and healed. The future only looks as bright as the memories the mind recalls from the past.

Therefore, it is important to use the past as a guide to what you want and no longer want. The world is really a very friendly place if you know what brings you joy, who to choose as companions and playmates, and where to spend quality time.

There was a woman who telephoned me asking for my help with a problem she was having. When I met her, she told me she was basically happy, had a good job, nice friends, and a kind husband. For some strange reason unbeknownst to her, she would suddenly begin to cry. In the middle of the day and without warning, she would be moved to tears.

"Can you help me figure out what is wrong?" she asked.

In our work together, the two of us uncovered something from her past that haunted her. I asked her if she remembered day dreaming about her life in the future when she was a young girl and if she recalled what she hoped to do.

"I always wanted to be an elementary school teacher."

"Did you prepare to be an elementary school teacher?" I asked.

"Yes I did," she said. "I have a master's degree in education but I was so afraid of failing the national teacher's exam, that I decided to just not take it and save myself the humiliation of failure."

Many people live with an inner sadness because of the loss of a life dream or a life goal that has never been realized. If what we want to do with our life is very different from what we are doing now, and *the now* is not that fulfilling, sadness and even grief are natural responses. The unconscious has a blueprint for our continued unfolding in all areas of life. Imagination helps us to tap into the dynamics of that blueprint through dreams, daydreams, writing, and the profound questions we ask ourselves. Many of us have a strong desire to know our true purpose here and to understand what gives our life meaning.

I offered her a plan. She could put her good brain to use and study for the national teacher's exam by reading and joining a study group. She could use the imagery techniques I would teach her to mitigate her test-anxiety. She could draw on her inner courage to take these steps. As though Dorothy were inviting her along on a journey to see the Wizard of Oz, she jumped at the opportunity of working in this way with me. Suddenly, where she had been all these years and how long she had been there did not matter to her. All that mattered was where she was going in future time.

A few months later after we had completed our work, I received a letter from her with an enclosed photo. In the picture she was smiling surrounded by her elementary school students. It took her a long time, but she had finally found her heart.

Going back in time and revisiting positive memories is much more constructive than dwelling on unpleasant ones. While in present time, The Tin Woodman reflected on the past and recalled a time when he was in love. As he focused his thoughts and memories there, he recaptured the feeling of the happiest time in his life. He wanted to feel that loving way again and in order for him to do that he needed to get a heart. Once he had a heart, he could fall in love again.

The future we create is tied to the past we most associate with. If we mostly gravitate to dark and depressing memories, the present will tend to look and feel the same. The places we most frequently take our minds to in the past will color the present with either fear or harmony. As we get into the habit of drawing on positive and uplifting memories, we will see a future filled with hope, love, courage, and light. Time travel can be a life changing journey. Where the mind goes, what it entertains, and how long it stays there are extremely important to our present health and well-being and to the future we want to create. Paying attention to the places the mind travels to and learning to retrain it in the sojourns it takes is a valuable skill.

When the Lion tells Dorothy that he probably was born a coward, he is traveling back in time as he sees a sad and lonely picture there. That past picture creates fear and limitation.

What does a person look like born a coward?

What does a person feel like believing he was born a coward?

How would a person act if he thought he was a coward from the very beginning of his life?

What would his future look like if his reference point was that he was born a coward?

How we think of our past and the accompanying pictures and images that arise directly impact the present and the future. The Lion acts like a coward and that is why Dorothy slaps him on the snout. That slap is a wake up call for him to stop acting like a Cowardly Lion and to start acting like a Courageous Lion. As he begins to express his courage in small ways and big ways, his life is transformed. He no longer lets the past dictate how he is going to act now and in the future.

When we spend time thinking about the future in the imagination, we are moving forward in time. This occurs anytime we daydream, play with future possibilities, or imagine doing something on another day. Dorothy, the Scarecrow, the Lion, and the Tin Woodman are all going to Oz in their imaginations to accomplish specific goals. Each step they take brings them closer to their future dream of getting their wishes fulfilled.

We time travel like this all the time. When we look at a beautiful car and imagine driving it, when we look at a new home and imagine living there, when we meet someone we are interested in and begin envisioning things we can do together, when we see a picture of a beautiful coastal town in Italy and imagine being there in the future, we are traveling through time and seeing good things happen. When the Good Witch tells Dorothy that the Wizard of Oz can help her, that lovely voice inspires Dorothy to immediately see a bright future. A feeling of hope takes over as she sees herself safely back home in her imagination. When the Wicked Witch tells Dorothy that she is going to get her and her dog, that shrilling voice generates fear.

Traveling through time into the future can have both positive and negative results associated with it. Anytime we think about a bleak future, things won't work out in our favor, nothing will turn out right, an unfulfilling life situation will drag on and on, we are using the powers of the mind and imagination very unproductively. When Dorothy imagines she might be stuck in the Land of Oz and never return home, she moves into an inner place of fear.

These two processes, moving back in time and moving forward in time, always play an active role in the mind and imagination. They are fundamental abilities and their use will tell us a lot about the healthiness or unhealthiness of the mind.

The great Teacher, Yogi, and Spiritual Master Paramahansa Yogananda, was approached by a man who wanted to learn how to meditate. Yogananda clearly explained what needed to be done for successful meditation.

The man thanked Yogananda and prepared to leave when Yogananda said to him, "I forgot to tell you one more thing. When you meditate, do not think about monkeys!"

The man thanked him and went on his way. Weeks later the man returned and angrily told Yogananda that once he told him not to think about monkeys, all he could think about was monkeys and these thoughts and images were impairing his ability to concentrate.

"Why did you tell me not to think about monkeys?" the man asked. Yogananda told the man that he wanted him to see how much control his mind had over him and how much control he had over his mind.

This story illustrates how powerful the mind is and how it controls the content of thoughts, images, pictures, concepts, and beliefs. A simple suggestion or remark can produce an immediate journey of the mind. The thoughts and the images we conjure either bring us joy or suffering. Our thoughts create the present and our thoughts create the future.

Yogananda always maintained a very playful attitude and manner. Play has an endearing quality, uses the imagination in creative ways, and typically draws us closer together. When funny things happen, we enjoy telling others these humorous stories. We love to play and we love to laugh. The problem is we don't laugh and don't play enough.

If you look in the dictionary, you will find that few words have more descriptive meanings than the word play. Play has more than a hundred different applications and ways of being expressed. In one of its most sophisticated roles, play serves an important developmental purpose. Play is instrumental to the process of socialization which includes psychological growth and physical development. You learned how to interact with others, made friends, increased balance and body strength, and developed self awareness through play. Playing was one of the healthiest ways your parents made contact with you. Some of your happiest memories of growing up probably are ones that involved play.

Play creates feelings of belonging and acceptance and teaches you about creativity, rhythm, boundaries, and freedom. Through play you learn about sacred and imaginary space, laughter, amusement, relaxation, and the art of pretending. Play invites you to figure things out, use your head wisely, open your heart, and to draw upon your inner courage. Within the context of play, rules and a sense of order are learned. Play teaches you to use your imagination, take risks, move, run, dance, and sing. Through play and the magic of touch, you discover bodily pleasure and are awakened to a host of bodily sensations.

During a visit to her home, Elizabeth Kubler Ross told me a story that took place during one of her medical residencies. She was working at a children's hospital and for some unexplained reason, the children in one of the children's wards were improving more both physically and psychologically than children in the other wards. The medical staff met to try and figure out what was going on. Why were the children in this one ward doing so much better than in the other wards? The medical staff studied the children and their care in every way possible but they could not come up with an intelligent answer.

Elizabeth decided to visit the children's ward on the late evening/early morning shift. She found that one of the housekeeping workers picked up, lovingly held, and playfully rocked each child in the ward. One after the other, she played with them. The medical staff, interns, social workers and other therapists with all their combined education and expertise could not accomplish what the housekeeper accomplished through play and the power of touch. It became obvious to all that the vast improvement of the children was a direct result of the housekeeper's playful and loving manner. She did not have a college education and was not a trained professional, but she instinctively knew what the children needed. She knew how to enjoyably enter into the world of a child and play.

Many people see play in a very limited way. We have become a culture of couch potatoes. It is assumed that watching basketball or football night after night, yelling at the players and refs, and eating cookies and tortilla chips is play. Play is bigger, grander, and much more important to our mental, psychological, emotional and spiritual health than this.

When women are asked to describe the top five qualities they seek in a man, play is usually at the top of the list. Playfulness and having a great sense of humor are two of the most important qualities present in successful and fulfilling relationships. If the two of you cannot and do not enjoyably play on a regular basis, the relationship is probably doomed to failure or at the least, doomed to seriousness. It is this grave and serious orientation to day to day living that causes problems. Without laughter and a playful attitude, imagination struggles to find its way into our lives.

A friend of mine was having huge challenges with a woman he was involved with. They were seeing a couple's counselor together and each was also seeing a counselor alone. I asked him questions about play and then I asked him, "Can your inner little boy harmoniously and enjoyably play with her inner little girl?" As he thought about it, the answer was no! In his imagination he traveled back in time and saw a little girl that was often angry, demanding, stopped the game when she didn't get her way, picked up her toys, and went home. He was looking at the relationship in deep psychological ways but never really thought about how they played or didn't play together. He was raised with a very playful family, she wasn't. Play and maintaining a playful attitude are essential to developing intimacy.

If you didn't learn how to enjoy yourself as you were growing up, didn't develop a natural playfulness, and are still reeling from many challenges and disappointments that you experienced along the way, you may have the tendency to become much too serious. Many of the people that come to see me for help have forgotten the art of play and the importance of maintaining a playful mind and attitude. It is one of the most interesting things I noticed when I worked in psychiatric hospitals; the patients had forgotten the art of play.

Very early in my mental health career when I was hired as a Recreation Therapist, I was given the responsibility to work with eight patients on the intensive care unit and do something with them. I decided to purchase books on one-act plays and form a drama group.

The eight patients and I met weekly for a couple of hours and each patient read the part they had chosen to play. To my amazement, they rose to the occasion and assumed their playful roles with aplomb. This one-act play group helped them learn to focus, concentrate, and enter into healthy imaginary places with others. It helped them to see life from different vantage points, to step inside of another's shoes, and to safely communicate.

I took the patients out into nature at least a few times a week. Some of us were quite fortunate to be raised in an environment that permitted us to spend a lot of time playing in nature. Some of us were raised in cities with limited access to trees, flowers, meadows, and flowing water. Most of us spend too much time walking on cement, looking at anorexic architecture, listening to the sounds of noisy cars, and breathing in the pungent smell of polluted air. Most of us are nature deprived. Playing in nature helps us to relax, feel calm, and experience an inner state of tranquility. Taking long walks in the woods regenerates the soul. Taking a bike ride on a dirt road takes us back in time to being a kid again. Dancing on the water's edge invigorates the spirit. Spending time playing in nature rejuvenates our psychological, physical, and spiritual health.

In 1901, Richard Maurice Bucke, M.D. wrote a marvelous book, *Cosmic Consciousness; A classic investigation of the development of man's mystic relation to the Infinite,* in which he investigated the lives of those who he believed had achieved illumination and a relationship with the Divine. Included in those who he felt had achieved this state of consciousness was Walt Whitman.

Bucke wrote, "Walt's favorite occupation seemed to be strolling or sauntering about outdoors by himself, looking at the grass, the trees, the flowers, the vistas of light, the varying aspects of the sky, and listening to the birds, the crickets, the tree-frogs, the wind in the trees, and all the hundreds of natural sounds. It was evident that these things gave him a feeling of pleasure far beyond what they give to ordinary people. Perhaps, indeed, no man who ever lived liked so many things and disliked so few as Walt Whitman. All natural objects seemed to have a charm for him; all sights and sounds, outdoors and indoors, seemed to please him."

Perhaps we don't take the time to play because we believe we don't have time or because we are too self conscious. How can we play and let ourselves enjoy the simple things in life if we are worried about what other people are thinking of us?

In his ground breaking book, *The Farther Reaches of Human Nature*, Abraham Maslow wrote, "In what we call a normal adult adjustment, what has been described very nicely as being able to get along well in the world, being realistic, common sense, being mature, taking on responsibility, we have given up our poetry, our imagination, our softness, our childishness, our fantasy."

The imagination is the playground for seeing the self in action. The brain does not know the difference between walking in the woods and walking in the woods using all your senses in the imagination. The brain does not know the difference between jumping in a pool and swimming with the dolphins and imagining you are in the pool swimming with the dolphins. In both situations, the same brain chemistry is released leading to feelings of pleasure, fulfillment, and excitement. The body just goes along for the ride. If you are unable to get out in nature as often as you would like, going to places in nature in your mind and imagination and vividly seeing yourself there can give you the same benefit. Where the mind goes the body will follow.

The 2000 Olympics is a good example of playing with the mind and imagination and seeing the self being successful in future time. The American women's diver, Laura Wilkinson, won the gold medal. She was in 8th place at one stage of the competition and then began to dive perfect 10s. One dive after another moved Laura Wilkinson closer to the gold medal. Finally, she overtook the two Chinese divers and won the gold. When asked by a journalist how she was able to mobilize her diving skills and tenaciously achieve first place, Wilkinson said that she remembered what helped her in practice and she began to visualize herself diving perfectly. She imagined that the judges were all holding up cards with a 10 on them and the crowd was applauding enthusiastically. When asked how she was able to practice months earlier with a broken ankle, Wilkinson told the reporter that she dove each day in her imagination. She used the power of end-result imagery; imagery based in future time, to successfully win the gold medal.

The imagination is a remarkable faculty to draw upon again and again even in the most difficult circumstances. When coming upon the great ditch, the Lion envisioned himself leaping over it with great ease. When seeing the oncoming swarm of bees, the Scarecrow envisioned pulling out his straw and covering Dorothy and Toto to protect them from their stings. Like the four of them, we can creatively move beyond each barrier life presents by envisioning moving beyond the obstacle, moving under it, moving over it, going around it, or dissolving it in someway. Using the powers of the imagination and intuition, we can use the mind to successfully see beyond whatever is obstructing our path.

Intuition takes the complications of life and reduces them to their simplest form. This is one of the charming qualities of *The Wizard of Oz:* it is a very simple tale that is filled with wisdom and magic. Intuition has the quicksilver ability to clearly see the answer to a situation which appears very complex. This is called an intuitive flash because it happens in a millisecond. Dorothy and her friends open the channel to their intuitive wisdom again and again as they travel along the yellow brick road. Intuition has many levels of expression: physical, emotional, intellectual, and spiritual.

Opening and activating the inner power of intuition allows us to see with more watchful eyes, to hear with more observant ears, to touch life with greater sensitivity, and to feel with deeper and more fulfilling passion. Opening to these inner realms of the psyche and seeing the vast possibilities there transforms ordinary life into an extraordinary experience.

We can use the mind and imagination creatively to focus on future imagery that symbolizes peacefulness, empowerment, achievement, and success. We can let these inner pictures become a source of inspiration for us, awakening possibilities of how exciting and rewarding life can become by experiencing new heights of achievement in future time.

The story of Alfred Nobel is a case in point. Alfred Nobel was a very successful chemist and engineer who, quite by accident, mixed two substances together that had never been mixed together before, and as a result he discovered dynamite. This explosive became so popular that within a ten year period, Nobel had dynamite factories in twenty countries. Nobel became very wealthy as a result of the huge sale of dynamite but he didn't realize that dynamite was going to be used for destructive purposes and that many innocent people would die because of its use. He originally envisioned it being used to mine coal and precious metals and to move large sections of earth to create waterways.

In the late 1880's his brother died, but one of the French newspapers mistakenly put Alfred's name in the obituary. He was called the 'Angel of Death' for the thousands who had been killed as a result of his dynamite. When Alfred read his own obituary, he was shocked to see how he was going to be remembered when he actually did die! In a single moment, his entire past and future crossed his mind and he intuitively knew he had to make a change. "What do I want to be remembered for?" he mused.

In time traveling to the future, his imagination came up with the grand vision of awarding $1,000,000.00 in prize money each year to five people in the world who made the greatest discoveries and did the most important work in Physics, Medicine, Chemistry, Literature, and some aspect of World Peace. Alfred Nobel reinvented himself due to an error. His legacy is the creation of the Nobel Prizes. The Nobel Prizes continue to be offered over

100 years later and are regarded as the most prestigious awards in the world.

Alfred Nobel was looking for his brother's name in the obituary section of the newspaper to see what the reporter had to say. Transfixed by what he read and deeply saddened by what his life had become, he immediately knew he had to make sweeping professional changes. He began to envision what he wanted his future and legacy to look like. The amazing thing about this story is that there were many choices he could have made as a result of the paper's error. He could have ignored the article in the paper. He could have become furious with what was said and never change. He could have gone into a deep depression over the past mistakes he had made. Like Dorothy, he chose to transform the situation he found himself in. He became a Wizard of Light rather than being remembered as Wizard of Death. Like the Scarecrow reinventing himself, Nobel became a visionary and used his mind and imagination creatively rather than destructively. Like the Tin Woodman, Nobel did something that had a heart. And like the Lion, Nobel courageously expanded the scope of his business world, leaving behind the restrictive life he once identified with.

Nobel acknowledged five people each year who had 'a brain' and used their minds in remarkable ways. He brought world recognition to five people who had 'the courage' to take risks in their respective areas of passion. He honored five people who had 'a heart' and who made the world a better place because of their reverence for life.

Time traveling to the future is an exhilarating process that can also be used successfully to create images of health and well-being. Using the mind and imagination in this way was the goal of a Nurse who came to see me. She was scheduled for surgery and wanted to make the surgery and her recovery from the surgery hugely successful. 'Hugely successful' meant that she would go into the surgery with a positive outlook, knowing and seeing the surgeon's hand in future time performing a perfect surgery without a single complication. It also meant that her recovery would be quick and her pain minimal. In addition, it meant that there would be virtually no swelling.

Cheryl was born with a genetic condition adversely affecting the bone in her jaw. This, along with other complications, resulted in her having many dental surgeries starting when she was just a little girl. Each dental procedure seemed to get worse and each recovery period seemed to be longer and more arduous. She wanted to believe that using her mind, imagination, and positive imagery would result in her having a complication-free post surgical experience.

I saw her on a Saturday, and the following Thursday, just five days later, was the day of her scheduled surgery. She wanted to make an appointment to see me the Saturday after the surgery, which was only two days following what her doctor had told her was going to be a major procedure. I asked her if she wanted to wait a little longer to see me. Perhaps she needed a little more time.

"We've been using these relaxation processes and working on all these future images of a perfect and virtually pain free dental procedure with a phenomenally quick recovery time. I am feeling optimistic and calm. Why wouldn't I come two days after the surgery?" she said.

On the Saturday following her jaw surgery she walked into my office, sat down and looked at me with a twinkle in her eye. Cheryl had no visible signs of swelling or discomfort. She looked totally normal! "Did she cancel the surgery?" I mused.

In fact, she had the procedure and it turned out exactly as she had envisioned it. Working in the nursing profession, she now specializes in helping others use their minds and imaginations in the process of healing. Her surgery was so successful because she saw her future in a different light and felt much more relaxed and hopeful about the end result. The power of positive suggestion helped her to think and talk differently. She no longer used her painful past experiences as her reference point for what the future could be.

All healing takes place in a relaxed state. Relaxation puts things into a new perspective. When you are calm, you can respond in healthier ways and make better decisions. Like the rocking motion of Dorothy's house in the storm, your breathing cycle has a very calming rhythmic motion to it. If you pay close attention to the natural rhythm of your breath going in and going out, make an effort to slow down the in-breaths and out-breaths, you will notice yourself become increasingly more relaxed. Like Dorothy and Cheryl, it behooves you to sit calmly despite whatever is going on in your life. Nothing is going to improve when you are upset. Being in a panicked state of mind is not going to help you make a better decision. But things will change for the better when you are relaxed. You can think more clearly when you are relaxed and assess things in a more balanced way. And, most importantly, when the mind is calm, the imagination is freed.

Dorothy, the Scarecrow, the Tin Woodman, the Lion, Cheryl, Laura Wilkinson, and Alfred Nobel, all did the same thing with their imaginations as they traveled into future time and played with the possibilities there:

"I am going home!"

"I am going to get a brain!"

"I am going to get a new heart and love again!"

"I am going to get courage!"

"I am going to have a perfect and pain-free surgery!"

"I am going to dive perfect 10s!"

"I am going to create the Alfred Nobel Prizes for excellence!"

What these seven dear souls had in common is that they were able to 'reframe' their current experience by turning it into something else, and that something else was a precious gift. Reframing is a process of creating a dynamic shift in perception which positively alters the way we see, think, and feel. It is a way of making the transition from seeing limitation to seeing possibility. It is a new habit we can develop that helps us to move away from focusing on what isn't working to focusing on what can and will work. One moment the Scarecrow is stuck on a pole and the next minute he is skipping with Dorothy on the yellow brick road to get a brain. He is no longer thinking about or talking about how long he has been stuck. His mind and imagination have shifted from where he has been to where he is now to where he is going. The past no longer haunts him because his mind and imagination are re-oriented. At one point in the Olympic Games Laura Wilkinson is in 8th place. When she finds her way back to her yellow brick road she creatively uses her skills and imagination to win the Gold.

This is not just folly. I have seen it happen in my classes thousands of times. One morning Cheryl was 'here' in present time reflecting 'back then' on her past history of surgeries, and from these two vantage points in time looking into the future 'there' with regret. Within a few hours she was 'here' in present time but now looking into the future 'there' with the anticipation of having a pain-free surgery. It is so exciting for me to watch this amazing transformation unfold right before my eyes, to watch people travel through time in their imaginations with an entirely different mind-set.

As we spend more time playing with the power of the imagination, we will probably find that we will want to naturally transcend our past and open to the beauty of the present and the possibilities of the future; to transcend everything that blocks our sense of joy, vitality, and fulfillment. The imagination can take us on a journey, like Dorothy, to distant lands and higher realms of consciousness by just closing our eyes, taking a few relaxing breaths, trusting the power of the unconscious mind, believing in what is possible, and letting the natural flow of imagery unfold.

With its visual, auditory, and kinesthetic delights, *The Wizard of Oz* touches the transcendent realm within each of us. Transcendence moves beyond the known to the unknown. Transcendence can take you to mystical, magical, and fascinating places within your heart, mind, and imagination. Together, Dorothy and her companions totally transform the Land of Oz as they transcend their pasts and create their futures.

The mind and imagination have the phenomenal ability to dramatically alter the course of our lives. Once we begin to trust in the power to heal our limited perception of things, we will never be the same. Dorothy, the Scarecrow, the Tin Woodman, the Lion, Cheryl, Alfred Nobel, the man crossing the border, and Laura Wilkinson, were suddenly and extraordinarily transformed. In their transformation and travel through time, they began to think differently, see differently, feel differently, and act differently. This transformation can be likened to the near-death experience. When we return from that other realm, our perception of life is changed forever. This alteration of consciousness is not just a gift for the few. Like Dorothy, the Scarecrow, the Tin Woodman, and the Lion, you too can return to the Land of Oz and find hope, love, and courage on your yellow brick road.

As I walk on my Yellow Brick Road,

I have an unlimited capacity to love, learn, give, grow, and be happy.

I am free to make decisions and to make choices which make my life fulfilling.

I am free to establish priorities which reflect my own inner needs.

I am free to be myself, to play, to smile, and to laugh.

I am free to spend time with people I respect and who respect me.

I am free to heal from whatever is causing me distress, anguish, or pain and free to let go of whatever is disturbing my inner peace.

I reach out and help those I meet along the way in anyway I can.

I ask for help when I need it and accept help when it is offered.

I know that I was created to love and be loved, to live a life filled with joy, passion, compassion, and creativity.

I am learning the wisdom of being easier on myself, releasing negative thinking, and listening to the right voice.

I spend time in nature, eat healthily, take good care of myself, and discover many new ways to relax.

I use my mind in amazing ways and open the door to my imagination.

I open my heart and I draw upon deep reservoirs of courage.

Bibliography

Baum, L. Frank. *The Wonderful Wizard of Oz*. Originally published in 1900. The Dover Edition, first published in 1996.

Blatner, Adam. *The Art of Play*. Human Sciences Press 1988

Bookspan, Martin. *101 Masterpieces of Music and Their Composers*. Dolphin Books Edition 1973

Bucke, Richard Maurice. *Cosmic Consciousness*. Dutton 1969. First Published by Innes and Sons 1901.

Buscaglia, Leo. *Love*. Fawcett Crest 1972.

Carlson, Richard. *Healers on Healing*. Tarcher Putnam 1989

Castaneda, Carlos. *The Teachings of Don Juan*. Ballantine Books 1968.

De Broglie, *Einstein*. Peebles Press 1979

Epstein, Gerald. *Healing Visualizations, Creating Health Through Imagery*. Bantam Books 1989

Frankl, Viktor. *Man's Search for Meaning*. Pocket Books 1963

Fromm, Erich. *The Art of Loving*. Bantam Books 1956

Gandhi, Mohandas. *An Autobiography*. Beacon Press 1957

Gelb, Michael. *How to Think Like Leonardo da Vinci.* Delacorte Press 1998

Gill, Derek. *Quest, The Life of Elizabeth Kubler Ross.* Harper and Row 1980

Harding, Esther. *Woman's Mysteries.* Harper Colophon Books 1976

Hawkes, Joyce Whiteley. *Cell-Level Healing.* Atria Books 2006

Jampolsky, Gerald. *Love is Letting Go of Fear.* Bantam Books 1981

Jung, C.G. *Memories, Dreams, Reflections.* Vintage Books 1961

Levoy, Gregg. *Callings.* 1997

Maslow, Abraham. *The Farther Reaches of Human Nature.* The Viking Press 1971

Mother Teresa. *A Simple Path.* Ballantine Books 1995

Myss, Caroline. *Sacred Contracts.* Three Rivers Press 2002

Paris, Ginette. *Wisdom of the Psyche.* Routledge 2007

Puner, Helen. *Freud, His Life and His Mind.* Charter Books 1978

Rogers, Katharine. *L. Frank Baum Creator of Oz.* Da Capo Press 2002.

Shames, Richard. *Healing with Mind Power.* Rodale Press 1978

Tart, Charles. *Transpersonal Psychologies.* Harper Colophon Books 1977

Tart, Charles. *Altered States of Consciousness.* Anchor Books 1972

Thomas, Bob. *Walt Disney An American Original.* Pocket Books 1976.

Von Franz, Marie. *Interpretation of Fairytales.* Spring Publications 1970

Von Franz, Marie. *The Feminine in Fairytales.* Spring Publications 1972

Warner Brothers. *The Wizard of Oz*, 1939

Wikipedia Britannica Online. Alfred Bernhard Nobel

Wikipedia Britannica Online. John Muir

Wikipedia Britannica Online. L. Frank Baum

Wolinsky, Stephen. *Trances People Live.* Bramble Books 1991

Zahourek, Rothlyn. *Clinical Hypnosis and Therapeutic Suggestion in Patient Care.* Brunner Mazel 1990

Breinigsville, PA USA
28 September 2010
246254BV00001B/1/P